SAILING
BACK IN TIME

SAILING
BACK IN TIME

A Nostalgic Voyage on Canada's West Coast

Maria Coffey & Dag Goering

whitecap

Copyright © 1996 by Maria Coffey
Revised edition copyright © 2002 by Maria Coffey and Dag Goering
Whitecap Books

Edited by Elaine Jones
Proofread by Lisa Collins
Cover design by Roberta Batchelor
Cover photograph and interior photographs by Dag Goering except where noted
Painting and sketches by Allen Farrell
Map by Catherine Hart
Interior design by Margaret Lee/bamboosilk.com

Printed and bound in Canada

National Library of Canada Cataloguing in Publication Data

Coffey, Maria, 1952–
    Sailing back in time

    Includes index.
    ISBN 1-55285-338-1

    1. Farrell, Allen, 1912- 2. Farrell, Sharie, 1907- 3. Georgia, Strait of, Region
(B.C. and Wash.)—History. 4. Georgia, Strait of, Region (B.C. and Wash.)—
Description and travel. 5. Georgia, Strait of, Region (B.C. and Wash.)—
Biography. 6. Boats and boating—Georgia, Strait of, Region (B.C. and Wash.)
7. Boats and boating—British Columbia—Pacific Coast. I. Goering, Dag.
II. Farrell, Allen, 1912-

FC3845.G47Z49 2002   971.1'3104'0922   C2002-910072-0
F1089.G44C63 2002

FOR ALLEN AND SHARIE
IN TRIBUTE AND WITH LOVE

■

CONTENTS

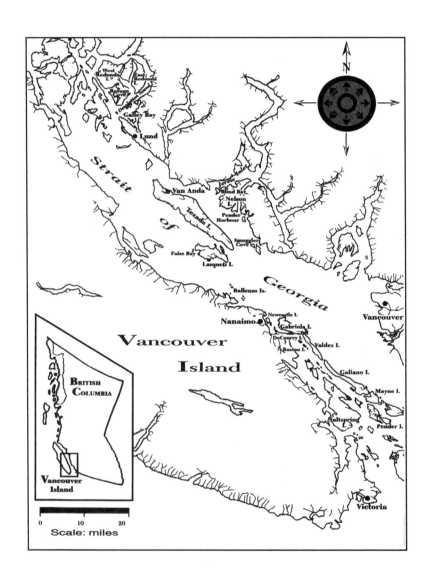

N

West
Redonda
I.
East
Redonda
I.

Refuge
Cove

Desolation Sound

Galley Bay

Lund

Strait

of

Van Anda

Texada I.

Jervis Inlet

Blind Bay

Nelson
I.

Pender
Harbour

Smuggler
Cove

False Bay

Lasqueti I.

Georgia

Ballenas Is.

Newcastle I.

Nanaimo

Gabriola I.

DeCourcy I.

Ruxton I.

Valdes I.

Vancouver

Galiano I.

Mayne I.

Vancouver

Island

Saltspring
I.

Pender I.

BRITISH
COLUMBIA

Vancouver
Island

Victoria

0   10   20
Scale: miles

PREFACE

■ Allen and Sharie Farrell have spent their lives on the coast of British Columbia, homesteading, fishing, sailing and building legendary boats from driftwood, and by hand. Now in their eighties, the Farrells still maintain a way of life that has all but disappeared from the coast. They remember it as a place where hardy, free-spirited people could make their living from the land and the sea. They have seen many changes and watched history unfold; a history of which they themselves are an integral part.

In the summer of 1995, Dag and I embarked on a voyage along the Strait of Georgia with Allen and Sharie, to revisit their old haunts and old friends. They led the way in their three-masted junk, *China Cloud*. We followed in *Luna Moth,* an open dory. Moving slowly, powered only by the wind and sculling oars, we sailed together through the summer, along a coast of incomparable beauty, and back in time.

This was an intimate journey, a sharing of the present as well as the past. It also marked the end of an era, for it was the Farrells' last cruise on *China Cloud,* before they gave her away and began a new stage in their lives.

During our voyage, we learned much from Allen and Sharie Farrell. They taught us the wisdom of simplicity. They showed us the beauty of living with grace and elegance, and without waste. And they revealed the possibilities that lie ahead in old age: adventure, romance and the realization of dreams.

CHAPTER ONE

Reunion

MAY 17 ■ We've been watching out for days, scanning the horizon to the north. At last, far in the distance, we see the sails: like tawny moths' wings against the eggshell blue of the sky. Slowly, slowly, they grow bigger. The late afternoon breeze is dying; other boats have doused their sails and are motoring in towards Nanaimo Harbour. But *China Cloud* continues to work her magic, moving with the merest breath of wind.

We watch, entranced, as she glides between Newcastle and Protection islands, the reflection of her oriental lines and rigging captured by the still waters of the channel. In the cockpit Allen and Sharie sit erect, staring intently ahead. Their eyesight is not as good as it used to be but, like so many places along the coast, this channel is as familiar to them as the palms of their hands, and they know its reef, its every rock and shoal, just as intimately.

MAY 18 ■ "When are we leaving, you guys?" cries Allen, as we climb out of our kayaks and hoist ourselves onto the deck of *China Cloud*. "Is *Luna Moth* rigged and ready to go?"

It's so good to be descending the companionway, and sliding into our familiar places on one of the benches flanking the drop-leaf table. Since they first invited us aboard, back in 1988 when *China Cloud* was anchored near our house on Protection Island, our friendship with the

Dag makes last-minute repairs to the copper sheathing on Luna Moth.

Farrells has steadily grown. They've become a touchstone in our lives, and their boat a haven of peace, wisdom and laughter. As we settle back against sheepskin rugs and soft cushions, my eyes run around the main cabin. A kettle steams on the old Fisherman wood stove, and the copper sheet tacked to the bulkhead behind it glows with reflected light. Some of Allen's small oil paintings hang on the varnished planking of the walls and larger ones are stacked on the floor. Books line the shelves beneath the portholes, and Mario the cat, as big and fluffy as ever, is stretched across a pink blanket on Sharie's wide bunk. I sigh happily. Nothing has changed since we last saw the Farrells, a few months ago on Lasqueti Island.

"Wasn't the winter awful?" says Allen. "I was cold all the time. Going to the beach to collect bark for the stove, picking it out of the snow— brrrr! I never want to be cold again. Next winter we'll be in Mexico."

He's already written to us about this plan. In the letter he sketched himself pulling Sharie in a rickshaw away from rain clouds and towards palm trees. "All the way to Puerto Vallarta" he'd noted underneath. Dag wrote back, asking if they wanted to sail *China Cloud* to Mexico and offering help.

"The thought stirs my blood," Allen replied, "but you forget how old we are."

I look at the octogenarians sitting across from us at the table. They exude so much energy and merriment, they take such a keen interest in the world around them, they have such young spirits and are so full of plans—how *can* they expect us to think of them as old?

Allen spreads a map of Mexico over the table, and shows us the places they plan to go next winter.

"Have you decided what to do with the boat while you're away?" asks Dag.

"We're getting rid of her, and all the stuff on board," Allen replies. "We're not coming back."

We mouth words, like two helpless fish, then shake our heads in disbelief. His cornflower-blue eyes gaze steadily at us across the table.

"There's so much work on a boat. I'm getting too old for it now. It took me two and a half years to build *China Cloud*. When I finished, I said, 'Well, if we live on her for two more years it will all have been worth it.' And now it's thirteen years later and we're still here. It's time for someone else to have the boat. We'll go to Mexico, find a place on the beach, maybe build a little dory. We'll be warm."

He pauses, and smiles apologetically. "Don't look so upset."

I glance at Sharie, who is sitting quietly beside him, her face giving little away. At last I find my tongue.

"*China Cloud* is your home, Allen. What if you want to come back? Why not go on holiday to Mexico and have a look around, before you burn all your bridges?"

He starts to chuckle.

"But I like burning bridges," he retorts. "I've done it all my life!"

M A Y 1 9 ■ My first thought as I wake: it's like being rocked in a cradle. I lie for a while, soothed by the gentle movement of our boat, by the lapping of water against the hull and the croaking of a raven deep in the forest on Newcastle Island. I think about the sounds of our house: the humming of the fridge, the ringing of the phone, the thump of clothes in the dryer. Last night we left behind those sounds, and the machines that make them. Our dory, *Luna Moth,* was moored outside the house. When the tide went out and she settled on the sand flats, we carried down food, books and equipment, and loaded her with all we needed for the next three months. We sat in the cockpit, our excitement mounting as the tide came in, swirling round the hull, lifting her off the bottom. Then we sailed half a mile around to Echo Bay, also known as Mark Bay, on the south side of Newcastle Island, and dropped anchor next to *China Cloud.* Our summer trip with the Farrells had begun.

A pale golden light filters through the ripstop nylon stretched across bamboo hoops over the midsection of our boat. Framed by the open end of this canopy is a jumble of honeycombed boulders, their undersides draped with glistening seaweed. A seagull hovers into the picture, drops a shell on the rocks to crack it open, and flaps down to investigate its contents. Gently pushed by a harbour breeze, the boat swings on her anchor and the picture slowly changes: to a pale blue sky flecked with pink clouds, to rabbits hopping across a meadow on Newcastle Island, to a loon dipping its head into the calm green water of the bay. Finally we settle, and filling the frame is *China Cloud,* smoke drifting lazily from her stovepipe.

I sit up, hugging my knees, gazing at the boat's exquisite details: the Chinese calligraphy and the dragon woman carved onto the hull, the curved cloud heads at the bow and the copper-clad rudder. A hatch is pulled back and Allen appears, his hair snow white in the early morning sunshine. He steps onto the centre well between the fore and main cabins, gazes up at the sky, peers myopically towards *Luna Moth,* then disappears again. Next to me Dag stirs.

"Breakfast?" he suggests.

We pull out food from the lockers under the seats of the cockpit and set the kettle to boil over a tiny alcohol stove. While I'm spreading peanut butter and honey onto bread, a family of Canada geese paddles up to join us. I scatter crumbs on the water, then hold out a crust towards one of the six tiny goslings. Its little feet work furiously as it dithers about, trying to pluck up courage to come closer. Then its father intervenes, stretching out his neck and hissing threateningly at me.

"It's blowing northwest again, but you don't notice it in this little bay," says Dag. Steam has started puffing out of the kettle, and he drops two teabags into the boiling water. "If the wind switches to southeast, we can move over to the gap between Newcastle and Protection, like Allen and Sharie always do."

He pauses, and stirs the tea. "I can't believe they won't be here on the boat next year. But Allen seems to have made up his mind, and I don't think he'll change it."

For a few minutes, we drink in silence, staring at *China Cloud*. I think about how enthusiastically the Farrells responded last summer, when we suggested making this journey with them.

"It will be like a holiday," Sharie had said, and Allen pulled down a chart from the shelf above her bunk, unrolled it on the table and marked with a black pen where we should go: the islands he'd fished off during the thirties, the places he and Sharie had built boats, the land they'd owned, the beaches where they'd dug for clams. Soon, there were black crosses all up and down the Strait of Georgia.

"Next May would be the best time to leave," he'd said, "and we should finish before mid-August, because it often starts raining then."

Did he know then that they'd be giving up *China Cloud?* That this would be their last cruise in her, perhaps the last time they travelled to some of the places he marked on the map?

A soft honking breaks my reverie. The geese are back, hoping for more food. I crumble a piece of bread between my fingers and throw it to them, careful this time not to ruffle any feathers.

M A Y   2 0   ■   By the alcove opposite *China Cloud's* galley, Sharie is looking into a mirror and combing her hair. Soft grey curls fall around her face. She's wearing a long wraparound skirt made of Indian cotton and a mauve t-shirt. Her tiny waist is accentuated with a colourful belt, and around her neck is a deftly tied scarf. This distinctive style changes little with the seasons. In the winter she'll add layers—a fluffy angora sweater, a beret—but never anything bulky or unfeminine. I've yet to see her wearing pants, except in an old photograph. Once, when I suggested she should get a pair for the winter, Allen had scowled at me.

"You look lovely, Sharie," I tell her, but she shakes her head in disbelief.

"She was just complaining about her skin being all lines and patches," says Allen. "I keep telling her she's beautiful, she could pass for twenty-five."

"Oh honey," murmurs Sharie.

"Well then," he concedes, "thirty-two. Honey, you don't see yourself as I do, up on deck in your lovely skirts, so slender and graceful. You're beautiful!"

By now Sharie is covered with embarrassment, but she's saved from more compliments by a knock on the hull. Allen pops his head out of the hatch.

"Dale!" we hear him cry. "Come aboard!"

The man who descends into the cabin is big, handsome and sun-weathered, and wears a cap set at a jaunty angle. Dale Nordlund, who has just arrived from Washington aboard his boat, *Aegean,* is an old friend of the Farrells. They first met in 1956, when he sailed into Blind Bay on Nelson Island and came across Allen and Sharie, stark naked, building a breakwater for their dock.

"We've been friends ever since," he says, smiling.

As Allen tells him of their plans to give up the boat and move to Mexico, he continues to smile.

"Allen, a big rubber band attaches you to this coast," Dale says finally. He reminds him of the times he left British Columbia before, for the South Pacific, Mexico and Hawaii. "You always got homesick. You can only go so far before the band starts pulling you back."

"This time," says Allen, wagging a finger at him, "it will be different. You wait and see."

MAY 21 ■ The high-pressure system that's been sitting over the coast for weeks prevails, and a steady northwest wind blows day and night.

"A northwester's so cold and unpredictable," says Allen, gazing across the harbour. "It's got too many positive ions. That's what's making these people so frantic."

The Victoria Day weekend is getting into full swing. Boats are streaming in, their skippers vying for anchorages that will give them a

China Cloud's *bilge keels allow her to go aground at low tide.*

good vantage point for tonight's fireworks display in Nanaimo. *Luna Moth,* with her flat bottom, and *China Cloud,* with two bilge keels and a draft of only two feet ten inches, are tucked away into Echo Bay, closer to the shore than any of the other boats dare venture. I feel as if we're a vestige of the past: our wooden boats, with their copper-clad hulls, have no engines, no glowing computerized panels, no automatic pumps. Solar panels are their only concession to modernization. Out there in the harbour is the present and the future: fibreglass sailing boats and sleek motor cruisers, their generators rumbling while the ice for Happy Hour is made; jet skis zipping about; float planes taking off and landing; a helicopter whup-whupping overhead; rock music blaring from the fairground in Swa-y-Lana Park.

"Nanaimo used to be such a quiet little place!" wails Allen.

He and Sharie first came here together aboard *Wind Song,* in the late 1940s. Nanaimo's population was then around six and a half thousand, and its coal industry was in decline. The deposits discovered in 1849 were beginning to peter out, and the mines, which had supplied the British fleet in the Pacific, and exported coal as far afield as Hawaii and Russia, were closing down.

Aboard Wind Song, *1951.*

"It was peaceful here," says Allen. "Just horse shit on the roads. No planes or outboards in the harbour. Some of the trollers had got Easthope engines but they sounded nice, like this"—screwing up his face and pursing his lips, he imitates an Easthope engine—"Tuka-tuka-tuka-tuka-tuka-TUKA!"

He leans back, looking tired. Both he and Sharie are suffering from an intestinal upset. Suspicious of conventional medicine and doctors, Allen has decided to starve out the bugs, and has not eaten since yesterday. Sharie is refusing to follow the same cure—she has a voracious appetite and a fast of three hours is more than enough for her. She's also more stoical about her condition.

"When Allen's ill," she tells me, "he's always convinced he has some terrible ailment, like cancer, and that he's about to die."

"See these, Maria?" he says, pointing to the deep wrinkles running horizontally across his forehead. "They're worry lines. I was born with them!"

■

As night falls, *China Cloud* becomes a black silhouette. Beyond her, the colourful city lights are reflected in the calm water of the harbour. At 11:00 p.m sharp, fireworks begin. Rockets of sparkling light shoot up into the sky and explode into bright suns and dazzling meteors. Allen and Sharie are unaware of the excitement—they went to bed at nine as usual, and are too hard of hearing to be disturbed by the explosions of the fireworks, or the raucous pop music that follows them.

M A Y 2 2 ■ Sharie loves books, but since she had glaucoma in 1982, her eyesight has been steadily worsening. Allen usually reads to her every day, but this morning he's so weak from fasting that even focussing on a page makes him feel dizzy. They happily accept my offer to read aloud from *The Wreck of the Dumaru,* a 1930 edition that Dale Nordlund recently found in a second-hand book store. It's the Farrells' favourite kind of story, a true account of an adventure at sea. And it's made especially interesting because one of the characters, Frank (Freddie) Fredette, was an old acquaintance of theirs.

The *Dumaru* was a wooden munitions ship which supplied U.S. possessions in the Pacific during the First World War, and Freddie Fredette was the ship's carpenter. As it left Guam for the Philippines, the *Dumaru* was hit by lightning and blew up. Two of the three life rafts launched quickly made it to safety, but the third was at sea for twenty-four days. Half of the thirty-two men on the raft died of thirst and exposure, and two threw themselves overboard. The survivors, including Freddie Fredette, ate the flesh and drank the blood of some of the dead.

"We met Freddie in the fifties, down in the Gulf Islands where he was fishing with his half-native wife," says Allen, when I stop for a break. "He worked as a caulker and he designed and built boats as well; for a while he was at a shipyard in Silva Bay, on Gabriola Island. There were lots of rumours about the shipwreck—people called him the 'old cannibal' behind his back—but he never said anything to us about it."

The Farrells lap up the exciting accounts of storms, big seas and shark attacks. And the descriptions of the leaky old *Dumaru* and its feisty crew jog some of Allen's early memories. When he was a child his favourite book was Robert Service's *The Rough-Neck.* Its hero, Jack Moon, escaped his problems in America by jumping a ship bound for

Tahiti, where he became a beachcomber and had a series of wild adventures. The book inspired Allen, and he began dreaming of a seafaring life, of sailing to exotic places.

"So my dad decided to give me a taste of it. In 1928 he got me a job shovelling coal aboard the *Golden Sea,* a tramp steamer bound for Japan and China. For two months I was caked in coal dust and my skin was black. Our crew were pretty fierce. Once we had to lock up the cook for three days, because he was drunk and raving. I was the youngest on board and I was looked after by this big, burly Welshman. He took me under his wing and he said, 'If anyone touches this kid, they'll have me to deal with!' We had nothing to eat but salt beef and potatoes, and once a week we got a can of condensed milk and some spotted dick. I had no tooth problems until then— there was too much phosphorous and not enough calcium in the diet."

His journey took him through the islands of Japan, where he saw junk-rigged boats for the first time, and gazed in astonishment and admiration at their lines and sails.

"Did you ever think you'd have your own junk one day, Allen?" I ask.

He laughs, rubs his hand over his face.

"Probably. I always had so many dreams."

M A Y 2 4   ■   We're rafted up to *China Cloud* so that Allen can inspect a crack near the base of our mast.

"It runs across the grain, so that's not too good," he says. "It's not the wind that will break it, but the pounding from the wakes of those big speed boats. You'll have to try and keep away from them. But I think it'll last until we get back up to Lasqueti. I found a perfect mast growing there."

Now that the Farrells are feeling better, we've decided to head south, as far as Pender Island, where we'll visit Allen's sister Lois. From Nanaimo there are two gateways into the Gulf Islands. Dodd Narrows, a short, tight, deep passage between Mudge and Vancouver islands, has currents of up to ten knots. False Narrows, between Mudge and Gabriola islands, is wider, with currents up to only four and a half knots, but it is shallow and has treacherous rocks and shoals. Most boaters, in vessels with engines, opt to go through Dodd Narrows at slack rather than risk False Narrows on any tide.

"We'll take False Narrows," Allen decides.

"OK, I'll check the tide and current tables," says Dag.

Allen gives him an amused look. He doesn't have such tables on board *China Cloud*. He has a compass somewhere, but he hasn't seen it for a long while. The VHF two-way radio a friend insisted on giving him last year is shoved away in a drawer, gathering dust. He sometimes tunes into the weather reports on the radio, or the "worry box" as he calls it, but doesn't always pay heed to them, preferring to watch what the clouds are doing. Rather than depending on equipment and navigational aids, he relies on his senses and instincts, and is prepared for all eventualities.

"I think we should go early tomorrow afternoon to catch the slack current around three o'clock," says Dag, looking up from the tables.

Allen makes ambivalent noises. "Earlier might be better," he says. When I suggest we should listen to a marine forecast, he laughs. "Forecasts? I didn't know you were superstitious!"

CHAPTER TWO

Through the Gulf Islands

MAY 25 ■ Dag and I are having a leisurely breakfast and discussing what to do with the rest of the morning, when Allen comes on the deck of *China Cloud* and starts preparing to leave. First he stands beside the main mast, hauling on the halyard with his entire weight to hoist the mainsail. While Sharie holds the tiller, he weighs the anchor. To save his back he's made a special block that's suspended from the foremast, so he can pull on the anchor line without bending over. Then he raises the other two smaller sails, the foresail and mizzen. There's barely a breeze in Echo Bay, and Allen's tell tale, a red ribbon hanging from the top of the main mast to show wind direction, is hanging limply. Nonetheless, *China Cloud* begins to move, and ghosts by us.

"There's plenty of time, you guys," calls Allen. "Don't hurry!"

We abandon breakfast and scurry about. I pull in the anchor chain, hand over hand, careful not to chafe the edge of the boat. The anchor breaks the surface festooned in muddy seaweed, which I untangle and throw back in the water.

"Don't worry about that, get everything stowed away," says Dag.

Suddenly, we're both tense. As a novice sailor, I'm awed by how much I have to learn during this trip, while Dag is facing the challenge of keeping up with *China Cloud* for the next twelve weeks. Despite having all our three hundred square feet of sail up, we're barely moving, so he's working the yuloh, a long sculling oar which is our only other

China Cloud *and* Luna Moth *rafted up for the night.*

means of power. Rocking to and fro on the balls of his feet, he makes long rhythmic sweeps, slowly propelling us along. Meanwhile, I clear the aft deck of breakfast things, then crouch beneath the canopy, shoving our sleeping bag, mats, books, cameras and clothes into waterproof bags and boxes, and stowing these beneath the deck.

The wind is light all the way across the harbour, as far as the southern end of Protection Island. Out in Northumberland Channel, however, it is blowing twenty knots steady, and the waves are steep and cresting. Dag drops the centre board and tells me to pull aboard the little folding kayak that we use as a tender. This was easy to do when we were at anchor. Out in a choppy sea, on a boat that is heeling, it's quite another matter. After wrestling with the kayak for several minutes, I end up flat on my back like a helpless insect, with the kayak on top of me and waves rushing by only inches from my face.

"Come and sit on the weather side," calls Dag. He's perched on the edge of the boat, with the tiller in his left hand, and one of the sheets in the other. His hair is whipped back by the wind, and his eyes a. alight. "Isn't it beautiful out here?"

For a few moments I take in the soft contours of Vancouver Island, the steep cliffs of Gabriola Island, the dramatic snowcapped mountains on the mainland, and the sight of *China Cloud* ahead of us, running with the wind and steadily shrinking in size. Then a gust hits our sail, and water slops across the deck.

"Don't worry," Dag reassures me, noticing my alarmed expression. "We could go across the Atlantic in this boat. Just be ready to let go the halyard when I tell you."

Chewing my lip, I gaze at the three lines that are cleated down on the thwart ahead of me. After a few sailing lessons from Dag, I've managed to memorize their names and uses—the halyard for raising and lowering the sail, the snotter for holding the top yard against the mast, the hauling parrel for moving the sail backwards and forwards—but I'm still having great problems remembering which is which.

Hearing Dag curse, I look up from my examination of the lines. Traffic has materialized in the channel, and all of it seems to be heading for us: the Gabriola Island ferry, several fishing boats, a couple of motor yachts, a tug pulling a log boom. As their wakes meet waves, the water becomes chaotic and *Luna Moth* starts bucking about.

"Reef her down!" shouts Dag.

I lunge for the fattest of the three lines, praying it's the halyard. As I loose it from the cleat there's a sickening splintering sound from the mast.

"Quick—!"

The rest of his command is drowned out by a loud CR-ACK! In alarm, I drop the line, and the sail concertinas.

"Keep three panels up!" Dag barks behind me. "We can't just sit out here!"

With a drastically reduced sail area, we limp across the channel to the Gabriola cliffs. Allen has hove to opposite the log booms of the pulp and paper mill, and is waiting for us. He's sitting by the tiller, his straw Panama pulled low over his sunglasses. He leans forward to take the mug that Sharie passes through the small sliding window under the cabin roof. She appears on deck, holding the rope railings as she walks carefully towards the cockpit, and gracefully sinks down next to Allen.

the mast is getting worse," Dag calls to them as we

m not surprised, with that wind and the wakes from body power boats. If it stood up to all that it should be all right now. The wind is dying down and we can take it easy from here. Ready to go through the Narrows?"

The original Coast Salish name for False Narrows meant "go inside the back part." It seems a peaceful place, lined by old meadows, trees and some community docks. Dag explains that to avoid its reef and rocks we have to zigzag along the channel, first sailing close to Mudge Island, then heading over to the Gabriola Island side and aligning the two range markers on the shore. This might be straightforward, if we had an engine, if our mast wasn't cracked, if the current wasn't against us, if the wind wasn't gusting about. As the channel narrows and we approach the reef, a particularly nasty gust hits us from behind.

"Drop the sail!" yells Dag.

I lunge for the halyard, and release it from the cleat. Nothing happens. In a panic, I release the lines cleated down on either side of it. Still nothing happens.

"Drop the—"

"I've dropped *everything!*"

He lets go of the sheet so that the sail flaps about.

"Halyard's twisted," he says tersely. "Go and pull the sail down."

Scrambling under the canopy to reach the bow, I tug on the bamboo battens and yank on the sail, but nothing gives. Dag has no choice but to keep on precariously sailing, until the halyard suddenly decides to loosen of its own accord, and the sail drops.

By half past one *China Cloud* has squeaked through False Narrows and is waiting at the far end, almost a mile away. Just as we make it past the reef, the wind dies. The current is still against us and we start to go backwards. Then the wind picks up a little; but it has shifted and is coming, of all places, from the south—bang on our nose.

"Allen must have sensed this," groans Dag. "It's why he wanted to leave so early."

Three times over the next hour, we manage to tack past the reef, only to be pushed back again by the current. The trees on the hills of

Gabriola Island go one way against the sky, then the other way. Some people sitting on the deck of a waterfront house watch us, their heads moving from side to side as if they are observing a tennis match in very slow motion. On the beach, a plump man pokes about with a long stick while a dog sniffs around at his feet. I wonder if he might be looking for old artifacts, as False Narrows was once the site of Senewelets, a summer village of the Nanaimo Coast Salish people. Each spring they came here to fish, dig for clams, harvest camas bulbs and hunt sea lions and seals. A sizeable midden stretches along the shore. When the man bends to examine something, I'm tempted to call out and ask him what he's found. He looks up and stares at us, bemused by our efforts to tack into the wind and against the current.

"That was a success," Dag glumly quips after one tack, "we gained almost ten feet."

Finally, with the current weakening, we make it through the Narrows, and find *China Cloud,* totally becalmed and anchored between Link and Mudge islands. Dag yulohs over to her, and Allen throws out fenders and reaches for a rope to tie us alongside.

"Welcome to the goddamn Gulf Islands!" he cries. "It's always like this down here, the winds die as soon as you need them."

The Gulf Islands lie on the east side of Vancouver Island. Although officially they include Lasqueti, Denman and Hornby islands, north of Nanaimo, the bulk of them stretch from here down to Saturna Island. The name of this archipelago originated in 1792 when Captain Vancouver mistakenly called the strait between the mainland and Vancouver Island a gulf, which means a deep inlet with a narrow mouth. The naval hydrographer Captain Richards set this to rights in 1865, but by then Gulf Islands was an established part of the local vernacular.

"It's just like the Mediterranean down here," says Dag, gazing over at the shore. Above the rocky beaches of Link Island, shimmering golden grasses grow between crooked Garry oak and arbutus trees. The sun is beating down, the water is calm and glittering, and already I have the sense of being tucked away in a discrete pocket of the coast.

On *China Cloud,* Mario has emerged from under the table, where he retreats when the boat is under sail, and is sitting by Sharie's feet in the galley. She is brewing tea in a white pot with blue sailing ships on it, and toasting raisin bread on the top of the wood stove. Taking a couple of steps up the companionway, she reaches out to her "fridge"—a bucket of saltwater left in the shade on deck—for a carton of soya milk.

"We have to finish this up quickly," she says, passing it round for our tea. "It goes off in three days."

"That means it's good for you," chips in Allen. "Not like the ordinary milk they sell in the stores. It lasts eight days! If something doesn't go bad quickly, you shouldn't eat it."

Abruptly, he abandons his toast and goes out on deck. "Hey, you guys, the current is in our favour now," he calls down.

We hop onto our boat, untie and drift slowly southwards alongside *China Cloud*. The islands stretch as far as we can see, fading to a translucent grey-green against the horizon. The air is so still that from several miles away we hear the drone of a boat engine. Seals splash and snort close by, an unseen loon gives its unearthly call, a salmon jumps and slaps the surface of the water and tiny western grebes pop up right next to us. As evening draws in, we reach De Courcy Island. The smell of flowers drifts from its shores. In the dimming light, *China Cloud* is like a fairy-tale craft, with her big moth wings, smoke curling from her stovepipe chimney and the white-haired couple sitting at her tiller, playing a ukulele and singing old songs.

Now is the hour, when we must say goodbye,
Soon you'll be sailing, out across the sea.
While you're away, oh please remember me,
When you return, you'll find me waiting here.

We anchor for the night off the southeast end of De Courcy Island. Over supper Allen and Sharie tell us about their old friend Harry Roberts, who was shot at when he tried to sail into Pirates Cove in the thirties. The culprits were the members of the Aquarian Foundation, a cult based on De Courcy Island. Its British founder, Edward Wilson, was a member of the Theosophical Society. In 1925, during the craze for spiritualism and the occult that followed the mass bereavement of the First World War, he wrote a book which he claimed had been dictated to him by one of the spiritual beings supposedly guiding the human race. Adopting the name of Brother XII, Wilson came to British

Maria at work aboard Luna Moth.

Columbia in 1927 and set up the Aquarian Foundation. Using money provided by his followers, he bought land and established settlements at Cedar, six miles south of Nanaimo, and on Valdes Island, and then purchased De Courcy and Ruxton islands. On De Courcy, the Aquarian Foundation built a house and reactivated an old farm. Before long there were rumours of fraud, physical and mental abuse and rape, some of them put about by people who had left the cult. After police came in search of a girl believed to have been kidnapped, Brother XII built fortifications, armed the cult members, and instructed them to fire on intruders. By 1932, all but a few of the cult members had turned against Wilson. He fled De Courcy, allegedly taking a huge stash of gold with him.

Sharie remembers being on the Farmers' Landing in Nanaimo in 1949 and seeing a strangely dressed woman getting off a boat.

"She looked like someone from another age, in long black skirts and high buttoned-up boots. People told us she was from De Courcy and had something to do with Brother XII."

By then, however, all the members of the cult were long gone from the island, and the farm had been bought by German immigrants, two brothers and two sisters. The Wyss family lived a reclusive, strictly

Christian life, holding their own Sunday services. Their farm was self-sufficient—they kept a cow and chickens, tended the fruit and nut trees planted by Brother XII's group and grew a magnificent garden. In *Small Stories of A Gentle Island*, Ruth Loomis describes rowing from her home on Pylades Island to De Courcy one winter morning in 1959 and being met at the farm by a shy woman dressed in a long black skirt and sweater and a black scarf. She, or her sister, must have been the woman Sharie saw. When their brothers died, the women were stranded, as neither of them had learned to row, or work a motorboat. They sold up around 1964, and moved to Denman Island.

"Poor things," says Allen, when I tell him this story. "Religion never did anyone a bit of good."

MAY 26   ■   *CR-ACK!* Halfway across Trincomali Channel, as we tack into a stiff southeast wind, our mast decides it has had enough. *CR-AAACK!* It remains standing, but wobbles perceptibly. By now I know exactly which line is the halyard; I drop it, then scrabble along the deck and stare in horror at the mast's jagged fracture, opening and closing with the movement of the boat. And there's another, new crack, smaller but no less gruesome than the first.

"It's gone on both sides," I tell Dag.

"It's gone, period," he glumly responds.

China Cloud is already over by Valdes Island, dwarfed by its sheer sandstone bluffs. Not daring to pull up more than two panels of our sail, we hobble across the channel, and anchor close to a beach southeast of Shingle Point. Dag climbs into the kayak and paddles off towards *China Cloud,* which has hove to by Cordale Point, a mile south of us.

"We're pretty exposed here," he says as he's leaving. "If our anchor drags, be ready to jump out close to shore and guide the boat away from the rocks."

"Wonderful," I mutter at his retreating figure. "Just wonderful."

I pull out some hardtack and cheese, and boil the kettle for tea. But I can't enjoy my lunch. Waves are rolling in from the southeast, the boat is pitching about, and the mast is making alarming noises. Every few minutes I check to see if our position has changed. According to our map, there's an Indian reserve here, and I constantly scan the shore, hoping to see someone who can help me if the anchor does drag. But, apart from a river otter running along the beach, and an eagle circling the trees, I see only a couple of deserted shacks, some abandoned trucks and a trailer with its door swinging in the wind.

Two nerve-wracking hours later, Dag returns with the news that we're going to sail back across the channel to Whaleboat Passage, between Ruxton and De Courcy islands.

"Allen says it's a good anchorage because we can get out of it whichever way the wind blows. He's going to help me jury-rig the mast there."

Soon *China Cloud* arrives and we hoist two panels of our sail and follow her across the channel.

"The mast will be happier now than when you were anchored in that chop," calls Allen as he passes. He's right. Running with wind, we make fast progress despite our sail being severely reefed, and there's far less of the ominous creaking.

Once we're safely at anchor, Dag and Allen fasten a line to our mast with a series of half hitches, attach this to *China Cloud*'s halyard and start hoisting the mast out of its step. Leaving them to it, I slip into the water and swim over to Pylades Island. Scrambling onto the rocky beach, I step over a bright orange sun star left high and dry by the tide, and stretch out on a warm sandstone boulder. Across the narrow, dark green channel is Ruxton Island. Its shores are shadowy, cloaked with trees that seem to be hiding secrets. Errant members of the Aquarian Foundation were banished to Ruxton, and some, it is rumoured, were never seen again. From close by there's a crunching sound, and I turn my head to see a young otter eating a crab. Frightened by my movement, it deserts the meal and runs for cover, its narrow back slick and undulating. Farther along the shore, a great blue heron is standing in the shallows, motionless as a statue save for its chest feathers stirring slightly in the breeze. It makes a stab at a fish, its elegant neck and long beak instantly transformed into a lethal weapon. As I lazily swim back to the boats, the heron unfolds its wings and skims away, its raucous primordial croaking echoing off the bluffs of Pylades Island.

"Brrr!" says Allen, as I grasp the rudder post of *Luna Moth* and haul myself on board. "I just measured the water temperature. It's only sixty degrees!" Dag is hunkered down, using an old saw to cut off the mast just above the crack.

"It's Allen's saw," he tells me. "He knocked out every other tooth. It works brilliantly. I don't know why all saws aren't made like this."

"They used to be," says Allen. "When I was young the saws had bigger and fewer teeth. You know those six-foot saws they used for cutting down trees? They were called agony bars. Using them seemed like so much hard work. But they were much better than the chain saws today —quieter, easier on the nerves and far less dangerous."

The mast, now two and a half feet shorter, is lowered back into its step. Dag looks at it disconsolately.

"Don't worry," Allen tells him. "You'll have a new one soon."

Over dinner, which we eat together on *China Cloud,* Allen promises that we'll take things easy from now on.

"If the wind isn't right in the morning, we'll relax. I'll do some painting, clean up the boat, learn some more Spanish."

He takes out a Spanish grammar book that he and Sharie are working through, puts on his glasses and looks for the section they've reached. Sharie pulls on a cord hanging from the lamp attached to a beam above the table. A bulb lights inside the yellow lampshade, casting a soft glow over the cabin. A solar panel is a new and luxurious addition to the Farrells' life.

"We managed for years with candles," says Allen. "And we made oil for lamps from dogfish livers."

"*Dogfish* livers?" Dag and I chorus.

"Oh, they worked really well. We reduced them by leaving them out in the sun or over the stove. Then we put the oil in a saucer and dipped in a wick. It burned with a lovely soft yellow light, and there was no nasty smell."

Later, in the cockpit of *Luna Moth,* Dag reads by our hurricane lamp, which makes a gentle popping sound as it burns. I stare out from the circle of light to the darkness beyond. An owl hoots repeatedly from Pylades Island. Over on Ruxton, hundreds of frogs are singing, ending their songs in perfect time, as if cued by a conductor. As we swing on our anchor, the stars wheel and turn. One of them falls, burning out on its short, bright flight. I make a wish, climb under our covers, and am asleep in seconds.

Allen demonstrates the finer points of his back exercises.

M A Y 2 7 ■ What Allen calls a "dry southeasterly" is blowing at ten
knots. Despite his assurances of last night, by seven o'clock he's hoisting
his sails. We follow, and manage to reach Thetis Island before the wind
picks up. As it steadily increases to twenty knots, *China Cloud* comes
into her own. Pointing high into the wind, and barely heeling over, she
carves her way southwards. Poor *Luna Moth,* with a shortened mast and
a reduced sail area, is getting nowhere. When Allen realizes he's leaving
us far behind, he turns *China Cloud* and leads the way back towards
Pylades Island. On the way we're joined by a pretty little sloop, the
Mingulay, owned by Allen's twenty-four-year-old grandnephew Hans
Murray and his girlfriend, Pam Barber. A few days ago they set off from
Victoria to go cruising for the summer. From a distance they recognized
China Cloud and steered towards her.

"It's just as well we came back," Allen kindly assures us, when we're
anchored once again in Whaleboat Passage, between Ruxton and
Pylades islands. "Sharie and I hate beating into the wind. And now we
can spend some time with Hans and Pam."

Hans is the grandson of Kay, one of Allen's three sisters. When we
gather for dinner on *China Cloud,* stories about these sisters start to fly.

Allen tells us that every day, winter and summer, seventy-three-year-old Kay marches down from her house in West Vancouver and goes swimming off Dundarave Pier.

"She always goes in naked," adds Hans, "in full view of all those posh houses."

"Do you remember, Allen, the time she went swimming when she was pregnant with Sylvia?" says Sharie. "How old was she then—forty-seven I think. It was winter and she got really cold. She was so big and heavy she couldn't pull herself back onto the pier, and the people there called the police to help her!"

On their way from Victoria, Hans and Pam called into Pender Island to see Lois, another of Allen's sisters, and while they were there she got a call from Billy, who at seventy-one is the youngest sibling.

"You'll never guess what Billy's up to now," says Hans.

"Oh no," groans Allen, "I daren't think. When she was sixty-eight she did a two-hundred-mile bike race in two days. What now?"

"She's learning how to roller-blade!"

When Dag and I stop laughing, we explain to a puzzled Allen and Sharie what roller-blading is.

"Honestly, this family makes me feel old," says Pam. She leans forward and rubs her back, which is giving her a bit of trouble.

"Want to know how to fix a bad back?" asks Allen.

In rapid succession, he shows us a series of exercises. Lying on the cabin floor, with his feet hooked under the wood drawer, he does ten "crunches." Flipping over onto all fours, he humps and arches his spine and twists from side to side to look back at his hips. Standing up and leaning his hands on the table, he swivels his pelvis. Suspended by his fingers from the beam across the skylight, he does fifteen chin-ups. As a finale, he brings his feet right over his head and, while we all gape in astonishment, executes a controlled hanging somersault.

"In 1936 he won the B.C. championship for gymnastics and tumbling," Sharie proudly tells us.

Still hanging upside down with a bright red face, Allen cheekily sticks out his tongue at us. Then he slowly unwinds and lands lightly on his feet.

"Do that ten times a day," he instructs Pam, dusting off his hands, "and you'll never have a problem with your back."

M A Y   2 8   ■   We're woken at dawn by a squabble between a crow and a raven on Pylades Island. While we're eating breakfast, a rufous hummingbird buzzes our canopy, and a swallow swoops around the mizzenmast of *China Cloud*. There's a northwest breeze, but presently Allen comes on deck, gazes at the clouds, then shakes his head and goes below. Within an hour it's dead calm. When Hans and Pam leave, we hear the drone of *Mingulay*'s motor as she heads north.

Around midmorning, I pop over to *China Cloud* to visit Allen and Sharie. They've just finished their Spanish lesson, and Allen has written the words they've learned in large black lettering on pieces of paper and stuck these up in various places around the cabin. He's now working on an oil painting. It's propped up on an easel he's made by leaning the ship's ladder against the cabin table. Paints, brushes and a palette are scattered around him. Sharie is sitting on her bunk, sorting through one of the boat's drawers. Allen believes in drawers. On *Native Girl* he had over thirty of them. When he built *China Cloud* he increased the number to sixty-six.

"The problem is, we fill them up," Sharie tells me. "You've no idea how much stuff we've got to get rid of before we go away."

In the afternoon we all set off to Ruxton Island. Dag paddles the kayak, while Sharie and I go with Allen in the dory. He rows facing forward, "like all old fishermen," he says.

Ruxton's western shore is rugged and steep, and its sandstone bluffs have been sculpted by wind and water into bizarre shapes and honeycombs. Gnarled juniper and Garry oak trees twist skywards from the rock, their roots reaching back into long crevices where it's said that native Coast Salish people once buried their dead. Thin strips of red bark are peeling off the trunks of leaning arbutus trees, to reveal the smooth, olive-green skin beneath. Mats of succulent stonecrop and roseroot hang from the lower parts of the bluff, and ocean spray, a bush once used by Coast Salish to make digging sticks, arrow shafts and spears, is blooming in fine white clouds. At the water's edge, smooth boulders are stained pale green, bright yellow and black by lichen. Clinging to their undersides are big starfish, deep purple and wetly gleaming.

We're on our way to visit Ted Long. The Farrells met him sixteen years ago in Hawaii when they were on *Native Girl* and he was sailing

Salal, a thirty-one-foot Golden Hind boat. From the bay where we go ashore, a steep dirt path leads through the forest towards his house. As usual, Allen walks barefoot, oblivious to the sharp stones. Sharie, who is unsteady on her feet these days, uses a staff, and Allen holds her firmly by the hand. She stumbles often on roots and once she falls over, but in such a loose, relaxed way that she doesn't hurt herself.

"It's all the dancing she's done in her life," says Allen, helping her up. "It kept her supple."

We come to a sunny clearing among the trees. Neat vegetable plots are arranged in front of a charming little house with vertical log walls and a shake roof. In its wide double doorway, a man with flowing white hair and a neatly trimmed beard sits in a chair, leaning forward and staring so intently at the ground that he doesn't see us until we're almost upon him.

"Allen! Sharie! Good heavens!" he cries at last, leaping to his feet. Although Ted Long left the south coast of Britain for Canada in 1949, he still speaks with a strong Worthing accent.

"I'm sorry I didn't notice you. I've been watching these ants for hours." He points to a small rock wall and a line of ants running from it. "All day they've been moving their nest over to the wood pile. I've calculated that the equivalent distance for humans would be from Toronto to Vancouver. I haven't worked out the equivalent weight of what each of them is carrying, but it must be pretty heavy. If people worked like that the world would be all right—we'd all be too tired to make any trouble."

Ted, at almost seventy, is as industrious as an ant himself. He bought this land in 1991, and set to work building the house.

"I was going to lay the logs horizontally, but they were twenty feet long and really heavy, and that's one hell of a job to do on your own when you're talking about seven-foot-high walls. Then Allen suggested looking for seven-foot-long logs on the beach, and standing them up on their ends. I'd never thought of that before. It made perfect sense."

Ted is wiry and light on his feet. The sleeves of his sweater are pushed up, revealing strong forearms. To build this house he used no power tools, only a Swedesaw, an axe, a hammer, a brace and bit, a chisel, and lots of rope and blocks. The logs that form the walls were

Dane Campbell

Native Girl.

felled on his property or collected off the beach. The front doors were split from a cedar log two and a half feet in diameter. For a year, the only materials Ted bought were nails and spikes. And when the house was finished he started on a garden. He's aiming for self-sufficiency, and now has nineteen varieties of beans growing. He makes compost and uses buckets and a wheelbarrow to pack water for his plants from a nearby pond.

"The more labour-intensive something is the better, as far as I'm concerned. One of my neighbours asked me why I don't use a Honda pump to get my water up from the pond. I told him that working hard to get the water gives it value. See what I mean? This way, I never waste a drop."

He made every stick of furniture inside the house. He shows us round the small living area, the open loft reached by a staircase of beachcombed wood, the kitchen area behind the staircase and, finally, a tiny bathroom with a composting toilet.

"It's got a fan," he says proudly. "I run it off my solar panel. How are you doing with your panel, Allen? I remember when you first got it, I teased you about succumbing to modern technology and you said, 'Yes, Ted, but it's *so* quiet'!"

Sharie is inspecting the kitchen, which is neat as a pin.

"Is this to stop your cups and pots sliding off in a heavy sea, Ted?" she teases him, running her hand along the raised lip of the counter.

"I'd been living on boats since 1972 when I built this place," he explains. "I kept forgetting I was on land."

M A Y   2 9   ■   The rising sun, veiled in clouds above Valdes Island, sends out huge rays of light that fan across the sky, forming an ethereal backdrop to *China Cloud*. With all sails set, she's out in Pylades Channel, heading south.

"So much for Allen taking things easy!" laughs Dag, as we scramble out of our sleeping bag and set off in pursuit.

It's half past ten before we catch up with her, at the north end of Reid Island. There's only a light northwest breeze, the sun is already hot, and Dag is at the tiller, reading a novel.

"Now you know all about sailing," Allen calls to us. "You're either bored stiff or terrified!"

On the far side of the channel is Porlier Pass, between Valdes and Galiano, islands named after the Spanish explorers who were swept through the pass from the Gulf of Georgia in 1792.

"In forty-five minutes the tide will change," Dag tells me, "and if we don't get south in a hurry we could be sucked out into the strait." He pulls out the tiller, unties the yuloh and begins to scull.

We spend the afternoon slowly drifting south. Wind stirs up the water several miles to the north, but never reaches us.

Allen had hoped to reach his usual anchorage in Montague Harbour by this evening, but when the tide turns against us, we're forced to drop anchor at the north end of Parker Island.

"These goddamn Gulf Islands, they're always the same," he fumes. "We always get stuck."

Sharie is also frustrated by the lack of wind. "I've always hated drifting about," she tells me, as we prepare dinner together. "When we set off for somewhere, I like to get there."

We slice potatoes and onions, which Sharie layers in a cast-iron frying pan, sprinkles with flour, salt, and soya milk, and leaves to cook slowly over the wood stove.

"This is a wonderful pan," she sighs. "Allen wants to get rid of everything before we leave for Mexico, but I'd like to keep this. That's not unreasonable, is it?"

Considering she's about to give up her home and most of her possessions, I tell her, keeping one frying pan is not unreasonable at all.

After the meal I half-fill the small basin in the galley with water heated on the stove, add a few drops of detergent and start to wash up. A wooden shelf slides out from beneath the counter, and on this I stack the dishes to drain. As I work I think about how much water I use to wash up at home—a large sink-full, and the hot tap left running for rinsing. The average Canadian family uses between 250 and 350 gallons of water a day. *China Cloud's* water tank has a capacity of 110 gallons, which lasts Allen and Sharie several weeks. For a head, as the toilet on a boat is called, they use a bucket with a little saltwater in the bottom. To wash themselves, they heat up rainwater and pour it into a tin bath set on the cabin floor.

"Don't throw that away," says Allen, just as I'm about to tip the water out of the bowl and down the sink. "We might have some cups to wash up later."

M A Y   3 0   ■   It's still dark, but I hear footsteps on the deck of *China Cloud*. I nudge Dag in the ribs, and seconds later he's awake and up.

"Is there a problem, Allen?"

"Well, maybe. I think we're dragging. We're almost on top of the reef."

Dag helps him check the anchor. Everything seems to be fine, but Allen is too anxious to get back to sleep. We set off into a light southwest wind. The sun won't peek over Galiano Island for another hour or two. Shivering, I bundle up in thick pants, socks, a hat and scarf. In the cockpit of *China Cloud,* Allen and Sharie don't seem to feel the cold for once, and wear only their usual clothes with light sweaters on top.

By seven o'clock, the wind is still light and the tide is flooding. We sail to and fro south of Collison Point, wondering what to do. To get to Pender Island we have to cross Swanson Channel, and the mouth of Active Pass, infamous for its treacherous currents and its traffic. From behind Helen Point on Mayne Island, large B.C. ferries headed for

Vancouver Island swing out and barrel across Swanson Channel at about twenty knots.

"This is not the best place to develop engine trouble or to run out of wind," I read out to Dag from the *Cruising Guide*.

"At least there's no chance of us having engine trouble," he comments wryly.

On *China Cloud* Allen seems hesitant, holding the boat back.

"What do you think, Allen?" calls Dag.

Allen shrugs. He looks profoundly worried.

"We might as well go. But I don't know what's to become of us."

Still he waits, and so do we. Two ferries go by, one coming from Vancouver, the other from Swartz Bay.

"There won't be another ferry for a while," calls Dag. "Let's go for it, Allen." As we begin to head across the channel, erratic currents swirl around our hull, and we feel *Luna Moth* shift about. Dag glances worriedly back at *China Cloud,* which is still sailing to and fro.

"Come on, Allen," he mutters to himself.

Two more ferries go by, both making a wide arc around the light beacon on Enterprise reef.

"We'll head straight for the reef," says Dag, "and once we're close to it we'll be out of the path of the ferries."

I gaze down Swanson Channel, towards the haze wreathing the blue slopes of Vancouver Island. A white dot emerges from it, and grows quickly, steadily bigger, gleaming in the sunlight.

"Another ferry's on the way," I tell Dag.

"No problem," he reassures me. "It will change direction soon to avoid the reef." Helped by the flooding current, we make good progress towards Enterprise reef. The bow of the approaching ferry cuts cleanly through the water, throwing off a large, white wave on either side of it.

"Dag, it's coming straight for us."

"It will veer off soon. It can't risk getting close to the reef. Stop worrying."

Behind us, *China Cloud* still sails back and forth between Collison Point and Prevost Island. I imagine Allen watching us through binoculars, biting his lip. The ferry continues to loom, all five thousand tons and four hundred feet of it. The throbbing of its engines fill the air.

There are no warning blasts of the horn. Perhaps Dag is right, I think desperately, perhaps the ferry will start to swing at any moment. By now its bow waves seem enormous. I stare at them in mesmerized horror for a few seconds and then I snap.

"It's not changing direction!" I scream.

Dag pushes down hard on the tiller, and we come about.

"He was just doing that to make a point, I had right of way, look how close he is to the bloody beacon," fumes Dag.

As the ferry steams across what would have been our path, surprised faces peer at us through the windows. While we bucket about in its wake, Dag stands on the transom, shaking his fists and yelling something at the ferry, but his words are drowned out by the thundering of the engine. Finally the skipper sounds the horn—one long ear-splitting blast, which seems to emanate from the vessel's large and fast-retreating backside.

In the safety of Navy Channel, which separates Mayne from North Pender Island, where Allen's sister Lois lives, we make slow tacks, keeping an eye behind us for *China Cloud*. When the current changes, threatening to sweep us back into Swanson Channel, we drop anchor in Davidson Bay, known locally as Clam Bay, and snooze for a while, hoping to be wakened by Allen and Sharie's arrival. By late afternoon there is still no sign, so we sail back into the channel and head for Hope Bay, which is Allen and Sharie's destination on Pender Island. The bay is named after the family of one of the island's first white settlers. David Hope and Noah Buckley preempted the northern end of Pender in 1878 and split it between them. When Hope died a few years later, his property was inherited by some of his Scottish relatives, the Auchterlonies, and their daughter Elizabeth was quickly married off to an English immigrant, Washington Grimmer. It was a tough, isolated life for these early settlers. There was no wharf on the island until 1890, and until then animals being delivered to the farms had to be lowered over the sides of boats and guided to shore. Nor was there any medical assistance, and the Grimmers' second child, Neptune, was born in a rowboat, right here in the middle of Navy Channel, while Washington was frantically rowing Elizabeth to the midwife on Mayne Island.

Hope Bay is small and narrow, with old trees leaning over it and some decaying boat sheds along one shore. Dag manoeuvres the boat around the government dock that juts across its entrance. At his signal I douse the sail, and he deftly rounds *Luna Moth* up. Gently, she noses alongside the dock and comes to a stop. A man is standing at the top of the ramp, in front of a sign that reads "Galloping Moon Gallery."

"I have a message for you," he calls as we tie up.

"For us?"

"From Allen Farrell," he continues. "An hour ago he phoned my store from Montague Harbour. He asked me to look out for a wooden boat with a junk sail and a cabin like a covered wagon. He's worried about you. He says he'll come here when there's wind."

CHAPTER THREE

Pender Island and Back

MAY 31 ■ The morning is warm, sunlit, still. While we eat breakfast a turquoise dragonfly hovers around our heads, then settles on the yuloh, its iridescent wings outspread.

"The clouds are moving north," says Dag, gazing at the sky. "Allen and Sharie won't get far today. We should go and find Lois."

Along the road leading out of Hope Bay we pass an old wooden church, and a field where cows graze among buttercups and scratch themselves against gnarled apple trees. In a farm driveway, boxes of eggs are left out for sale, next to an "honour box" for money. The hedgerows are riotous with long-stemmed daisies, poppies, columbine, fragrant mock orange, honeysuckle and sweet-smelling wild roses. There are also large-leafed lupins, foxgloves and domestic roses, flowers which remind me of Britain.

"Perhaps the first white settlers brought the seeds with them," suggests Dag. As we stand and breathe in the heady scents, I imagine women at the turn of the century clearing and digging until their backs ached, planting the seeds, carefully tending the young plants and finally soothing their homesickness by setting vases filled with familiar flowers in the windows of their log cabins.

A passing car stops, and we accept the offer of a ride. I ask the driver if he lives here on Pender Island.

"I live on *North* Pender," he replies, a little testily.

Until 1903 Pender was a single island, with its two land masses connected by a narrow isthmus between Bedwell and Browning harbours. Then the isthmus was dynamited, and a canal excavated in its place. A bridge reunited North and South Pender islands in 1955, but they still retain their separate names and identities. Over a thousand people now live on North Pender, and although our kind driver has never met Allen's sister, Lois Flannigan, he knows who she is and where she lives.

"Her husband Peter was a legend round here. He was cantankerous as they come. One time they found him wandering round in his pyjamas with a shotgun under his arm, ranting on about how there was going to be a revolution. I'd regularly see him walking towards Hope Bay, right down the middle of this road. He reckoned it was safer in the middle than along the sides. There were signs all over the island warning drivers to watch out for him."

He drops us outside a gateway with a huge anchor next to it. At the end of a long sloping lawn, an Elvis Presley ballad is belting at full volume from a small brown house. Hop vines wind around the frame of the screen door. We knock hard, and shout. Abruptly, Elvis is silenced and a tiny figure peers out at us between the creepers.

"I thought you were my sister Kay, she's supposed to be coming," says Lois in a wavery voice. When we explain who we are, and why we've arrived without Allen and Sharie, she mutters, "Why doesn't Allen get an engine for that boat?"

Eighty-two-year-old Lois shuffles about her kitchen, making us tea. Her hair is wet, and she's dressed in sweats. Half an hour ago, she returned from swimming in the cold waters of Browning Harbour.

"I used to go every day, but now I've got a leaky valve in my heart so I only go on Wednesdays and Sundays. But I still do the Polar Bear Swim every New Year's Day."

She opens the fridge and stares into it.

"What did I want from here?"

"Milk?" I suggest.

"Oh yes, that's it. I'm a bit vague since Peter died."

All over the room, there are pictures of her late husband, Peter Flannigan. He was a tall, lanky man, with sharp blue eyes and an astonishing amount of snow white hair falling in thick matted ropes to below his shoulders. They married when Lois was in her early forties and Peter was close to seventy, and lived in a squatters' cabin on the Burrard Inlet flats, where Peter used to drink with the likes of Malcolm Lowry.

"Peter was a wild Irishman," says Lois. "Life with him was a battle. If I'd known how long he was going to live, I might not have married him. But I liked him better when he was older. We didn't fight so much then."

Peter was born in 1890 in Newfoundland. In his teens he ran away from home, and worked his passage on a ship bound for Portugal. During the First World War he fought in France, then returned to Canada where he worked on the railway and in logging camps, and became politicized through the left-wing Industrial Workers of the World movement. He retired here to North Pender with Lois, and became a renowned local character. One day he got talking to a tourist, and told her all about Conception Bay, where he grew up. She turned out to be a reporter from Newfoundland. On his behalf she contacted his relatives and a reunion was organized. At the age of one hundred, he went home with Lois to meet his family, eighty-six years after he'd left.

"It was on the television and radio," says Lois proudly. "The next year, we went on a cruise to Alaska. We'd never travelled before, so finally we thought we'd better hurry up. We wanted to go to more places, but he got too weak and then—" she pauses, and fiddles with her tea cup. "Well, then he just stopped breathing. He was a hundred and four and a half. I really thought he'd live to a hundred and five."

We sit in silence for a while.

"I keep him down in the basement," she finally continues. "But Kay's coming, and tomorrow we'll scatter his ashes, at Hope Bay. He liked walking down there. I hope Allen arrives in time for it."

She pulls out an old family album and shows us photos of Allen, handsome, dashing and with an impressive physique, in his early twenties. In one shot, he and his first wife, Betty, pose in South Sea Island costumes—a grass skirt for her, a garland round Allen's neck.

"He was always so romantic," says Lois. "Just like Dad."

She points to a photo of her father, Jasper Daniels, when he was a teenager, standing on the porch of an elegant wooden house in Nebraska with his brother Henry and their family.

"Jasper and Henry hated their stepmother, so they ran away from home and joined the U.S. army. They soon regretted it, and fled to Canada. That's how we all ended up here."

Lois and Allen, who was then called Mallory, spent their early years at the family homestead on Powell Lake. Jasper used to row the thirty-five miles to the nearest store, and often took his wife and young children with him. He worked as a fire warden, and also measured rain for the meteorological department. When he got a mapping job with the forestry department in 1918, the family left Powell Lake and travelled up the coast, living at various forestry camps on the way. After a few years of this, Jasper was promoted to an office-based job in Vancouver. The family left their life in the wilderness for a house in Dunbar Heights, and then in West Point Grey.

"But West Point Grey looked different in those days," says Lois. "It was all bush."

While she's looking for a photo of the house they lived in, the door is flung open. Standing among the vines is Kay, who we met about ten days ago in Nanaimo when she was visiting Allen and Sharie with her friend Larry. Several bulging cloth bags hang from her shoulders and she's holding a shopping stroller with a bunch of wild flowers strapped to the top. She's prettily dressed in a long skirt, a soft blue denim shirt and heavy silver jewellery. White curls escape from beneath her pink and white striped hat, and her sparkling eyes are emphasized with black mascara and liner. Her cheeks are flushed, and she looks impossibly young for seventy-three.

"We walked from the ferry and I stopped to pick flowers and a couple gave us a ride," she tells us. "Wasn't that kind? Lo, do you remember that singer who was a boyfriend of mine before I got married? I talked to him on the phone the other day. His wife is still alive but we made a date for when we're both a hundred years old."

"Which boyfriend have you brought with you today?" asks Lois, a mite disparagingly.

"Oh," says Kay absently, as if she's trying to remember, "Archie. He's picking your salmonberries. I'll go and get him."

While she's outside, Lois tells us that since Kay's husband died some months ago, she's had several admirers.

Allen and Sharie row ashore from Native Girl, circa 1970.

Allen Farrell collection

"They flock about her like moths round a candle. But she won't settle down again. Oh no, not Kay. She likes her freedom."

Archie walks in, smiling sweetly and extending an alabaster hand in welcome. He is small and stooped, with fine grey hair. He sits on a chair and watches Kay fondly while she flits about, pulling parcels from her bags and shopping stroller and spreading them over the table. When finally she plumps down on the floor and leans against his knees, he massages her head for a while, then starts pinching her cheeks.

"This stimulates her thymus gland," he tells me. "The best way is to beat her chest, but she won't let me do that. I beat my cat's chest every day, and she's lived to be twenty-two years old."

When we leave, Lois walks down the garden with us.

"We'll come to Hope Bay tomorrow with the ashes," she says. "I hope Allen and Sharie are here by then. Allen didn't talk to Peter at the end, you know. He was mad with him about something, but Peter could never remember what it was. The trouble with Allen is he just doesn't understand what it's like to be old."

J U N E 1   ■ In a moment of pure synchronicity, *China Cloud* appears around Auchterlonie Point and sails into Hope Bay, just as a car bearing Lois and her entourage pulls up outside the Galloping Moon Gallery.

"Did you plan this?" Kay cries delightedly through the window. "Were they hiding around the corner?"

Two of her daughters, Sonja and Marie, emerge from the car, clutching a small child apiece. Archie lends a hand to Lois, who has a brown plastic jar under one arm.

"Peter," she explains. "We nearly left without him."

"I had quite a job keeping these girls on track this morning," Archie confides to me. "They were like a flock of hens. While I was getting one in the car, all the others would escape and I'd have to go and round them up."

As *China Cloud* drifts into the entrance of the bay, we all hurry down to the dock, waving and calling to Allen and Sharie.

"Hello there!" shouts Sonja.

"Is that you Maria?" calls Sharie. "Are we ever glad to see you!"

"Honey, it's Sonja," Allen tells her. "What's Sonja doing here?"

While they drop anchor and start rowing to the dock, we mill about excitedly. Somehow I end up clutching the plastic jar of Peter's ashes, which is surprisingly heavy.

"Well, well, look at everyone here," chuckles Allen, helping Sharie out of the dory. "What's going on?"

"We have to say a prayer now, Allen," Lois greets him.

"A prayer?" His blue eyes are wide beneath his straw hat. "Whatever for? I didn't know you were religious, Lo."

"Maria, I couldn't sleep the last two nights for worrying about you," says Sharie, as I hug her. "I kept imagining you being run over by that ferry, and your boat in bits, and all your books floating around on the water."

"Sharie usually never worries about anything," chips in Allen. "So when she got so anxious about you, I thought, Oh brother! Maybe something did happen!"

Lois looks up at him, blinking back tears. "We're going to throw out the ashes now, Allen."

"So what, Lo? I throw out the ashes every morning."

"*Peter's* ashes, Allen!"

"What did Lois say, honey?" asks Sharie. "What's happening?"

"LOIS IS GETTING RID OF PETER'S ASHES," he shouts in her ear.

"Oh," she says vaguely, and gives me a quizzical smile.

Panic spreads over Lois's face. "Where's he gone?" she cries. "What did I do with him?"

I hand her the jar. She sets it down on the dock and Archie unscrews the lid for her.

"Poor Peter," she murmurs, running her frail fingers through the dust and the pebble-sized bits of bone. "All that's left of him."

While she contemplates her husband's remains, Allen and Sharie sit behind her on the dock, flanked by their nieces.

"One minute they were there," I can hear Allen telling them, "and then there was a ferry and they were gone. We rowed all over Montague Harbour asking if anyone had seen a dory with a junk sail and a canopy like a covered wagon, and no one had."

"Hadn't you better keep some ashes to take back east, Lo?" Kay suggests to Lois.

"Oh yes," says Lois gratefully. "You always have such good ideas, Kay." I race to *Luna Moth* for a Ziploc bag, which I hold open as Lois carefully tips in a quarter of the ashes.

"Shall we do it now?" she asks. "How does it go? Ashes to ashes, dust to dust, something like that?"

Kay puts her head to one side. "That one's a bit macabre, don't you think? How about, May your dreams and aspirations live on?"

"One fellow I talked to in Montague Harbour," Allen continues behind us, "he said the currents round here are different every day, sometimes going one way, then the other—the charts and tables don't tell you anything about them. Isn't that typical?"

"Allen," Lois calls to him. "We're going to do it now."

He gets to his feet, and with hands clasped respectfully in front of him, he stands by Lois's side as she begins to jerkily tip the ashes over the side of the dock.

"Bye-bye Peter," she says softly.

"May all your dreams and aspirations live on," adds Kay.

"Just dump them in all at once, Lo," advises Allen, then he turns to Sharie and calls, "You'll be doing this for me one day honey!"

The ash spreads over the water; bits of bone bob about. "He's gone," sighs Lois, and she gives a little wave.

"That was lovely, Lois," says Kay. "Very fitting. Shall we have the picnic now?"

■

Mario retreats to the deck and sticks his head through a porthole, gazing down in disdain at the nine adults and two children crowding around the table on *China Cloud*. Within minutes, a feast materializes. Dag and I make a salad, Sharie heats up soup, and from her bulging bags Kay produces organic grapes, corn, oranges, apples, bananas, yoghourt, cucumber, bread, and various spreads and relishes. Food is passed this way and that, and several conversations go on at once.

"Have you got children?" Kay asks me. "No? From choice you say? Oh, I think that's very commendable."

From across the table, Allen gives her a searching look.

"Don't say it!" she chides him. "I *know* the world is overpopulated, you don't have to tell me again."

She turns back to me, smiling sweetly.

"Birth control just didn't seem natural for me, so I kept having babies. Nine of them."

Allen is leaning forward, staring at her intently.

"What's that black goop around your eyes?" he asks. "You don't need that stuff, you're beautiful without it."

"Allen thought you'd been pushed down towards Sidney," Sharie is telling Dag. "I was sure you'd been lost without trace. It was awful. We'll stick together in future."

Lois has been sitting quietly, lost in thought.

"Allen," she suddenly pipes up. "Yesterday I told Maria and Dag about how Dad and Uncle Henry were born near Buffalo Bill's ranch."

"I didn't know about that, Lo."

"Didn't you? Ask Roe. He'll tell you."

"He's dead, Lo."

"Are you sure?"

"Everybody's dead now, Lo."

"I know," she laughs, her wry humour returning. "We have to pinch ourselves to make sure we're alive."

The party goes on until almost three o'clock, when Archie gently reminds Kay and her daughters that they have a ferry to catch, and should be leaving soon.

"I'm glad you can keep track of time," Allen tells him, "because no one in our family can."

They all pile into the dory, and Allen rows them to the dock.

"Look what they forgot!" he cries, when he comes back. "Typical!"

At his feet, in the bottom of the dory, is the plastic jar containing a Ziploc bag and the remains of Peter's ashes.

JUNE 2 ■ "Where's the post office gone?" wails Allen, clutching the letter he wants to mail. "What's happened to this place?"

He's standing in the middle of the Hope Bay Store, staring around the long lofty room. A gleaming cappuccino machine sits on the counter. On sale are herbal teas, incense sticks, crystals, gourmet chocolate bars, rugs and cushions from India, jewellery from the Far East. Such items are a far cry from what was offered by Mr. Corbett, who founded the store in 1905. His 1910 inventory included ladies' hat pins and high button boots, gunpowder and shot, kegs of cooking molasses, school slates and slate pencils, all delivered along with the mail by the SS *Iroquois*. In the fifties and sixties, when Allen and Sharie regularly anchored in Hope Bay, the store had a meat counter, a hardware section, household goods and groceries. Everything was delivered to the dock by the *Princess Mary*, which carried the milk from Pender Island farms over to the creamery on Saltspring Island. The arrival of these steamships was always a big social event, and the post office was a place where people met and exchanged news. Now, all that remains of it are a long wooden counter, scratched and shiny with use and heaped with second-hand books, a wooden frame for brown paper, string and tape, and pigeonholes for letters with hand-printed names beneath: Aggerholm, Aldrich, Alders, Auchterlonie.

Kees, the present owner of the store, explains to Allen that the post office has been relocated to the Driftwood Mall, in the middle of North

Pender Island. The mall also has a supermarket, a gas station, a bakery, a real estate agency and a pharmacy, and people drive to it from all over North and South Pender instead of patronizing the local stores. He now caters mainly to tourists, as do the art gallery and the gift shop in the old warehouse next door.

"You can't mail a letter in Hope Bay anymore—what's the world coming to?" Allen laments.

"It is changing, too fast," Kees answers sadly.

As we walk along Bedwell Harbour Road towards the Driftwood Mall, Allen grows glum.

"We used to be able to get all the way across the island on little paths through the woods," he says, "until everyone started putting up those 'Private' signs."

Today is a Friday, and the ferry traffic soon builds up. Cars whizz past us, and several times we're forced off the road and into the ditch. Soon Allen is growling with frustration.

"When we first came here people didn't drive, they *walked*. Bloody cars, it's them and war that keep the system going. The next thing will be America and Japan having a war over cars."

He trudges along in silence, holding Sharie's hand. As cars zip by, their drivers throw puzzled glances at the man with long, snowy white hair, walking barefoot with a large sack over his shoulder.

"This is awful," says Allen finally. "I feel like a ghost coming back."

JUNE 3 ■ In the middle of the night, a large fir tree fell from the bank of Hope Bay and landed in the water, missing *China Cloud* by ten feet.

"I thought it was an earthquake!" says Allen. "There was all this noise and Mario shot through the porthole, yowling. I looked out, and there were branches lying right across the deck."

We're standing on shore, surveying the tree. It is resting horizontally on some of its stout branches, which are impaled in the mud. A little closer, and some of them could have crashed through the cabin tops of *China Cloud*.

"We'd have been pierced through the heart," says Allen. "Not a bad way to go." He and Dag walk along the trunk, and disappear among its foliage.

A new incarnation for the Hope Bay Store.

"We always used to swim here and have picnics," says Sharie. She points to the remains of a stone walkway across the muddy shore. "Allen made that in the sixties. He made a wooden ladder up to the bank, too, but I guess that's gone now." Loud whooping rings out from among the branches of the fallen tree, and Sharie smiles fondly. "Apparently, when Allen was a kid he loved playing Tarzan."

■

Allen's father, Jasper, lived the last years of his life on an eleven-acre farm not far from Hope Bay. His old house, which we visit later in the day, sits above a field that rises up gently from the road.

"I remember this field on winter mornings, all covered by a lovely mist," says Allen quietly.

Jasper's brother Henry was the first of the family to live on the farm. After his wife left him for another islander, Henry died, according to Allen, of a broken heart. Soon, his widow was back at the farm with her new boyfriend. Enraged by this, Jasper arrived from Vancouver Island to throw the couple off the land and claim it for himself.

"He kept guinea fowl, about a thousand of them," Allen recalls. "They made an awful noise. And he used to dig potatoes in this field,

just with a spade. I suppose people use machines now. He'd been working here the day he died. We were anchored in *Ocean Girl* at Shark Cove
and he came down for a visit, then went off in his truck. He had the
heart attack while he was driving. He pulled over to the side of the road
and turned off the engine, so that he wouldn't hurt anyone. That's how
he was. One of the Auchterlonie men came to tell me that he'd had an
accident. I said, 'How bad is it?' and he said, 'As bad as it gets.' From the
way he spoke I imagined finding Dad all bloody and mangled. But
when I got there he was lying peacefully in the ferns."

We peer through the windows of the house, which is empty of furniture. Standing outside in the garden is a rusty old wood stove, stamped
"Dorco Laundry," with a mantle round its body for heating water.

"I suppose this was Dad's," says Allen. He points at the two plates on
the top. "Look, you put eggs and bacon here, a kettle there. That's all
you need."

Old farm implements lie rusting in the long grass. The barns are
empty and falling into ruin. When Jasper died, his estranged wife inherited the farm and allowed her daughter Lois and Peter to live there until
she sold up in the sixties.

"Poor Dad," says Allen. "He badly wanted me to have this place. But
I wasn't interested in land. All I could think about was boats."

J U N E   4   ■   Gerry Fossum is sitting in the main cabin of *China
Cloud,* looking as if someone has just hit him over the head with a two-
by-four. He recently wrote to Allen, asking for advice on a boat he and
his wife, Sharlane, have been planning to build. Yesterday Allen phoned
him and suggested he come over from Victoria for a visit. For eight
years the Fossums lived with their two children aboard *Native Girl,*
which they bought from Allen and Sharie in 1983. Before Gerry
arrived, Allen told us how lovingly the Fossums had cared for *Native
Girl,* and that when the time came they sold her to someone who they
knew would continue to cherish her. He also told us that as he was sure
his sons wouldn't be interested in having *China Cloud,* he had decided
to give her to Gerry.

"He's the right guy. He's emotional about her. He'll live on her and
sail her until he gets too old—like me."

"Why are you giving her away?" I'd asked. "Why not sell her, like all your other boats?"

"What would we do with the money?" he'd countered. "We get our old age pension every month, and it's more than we need. We've tried to send it back, but they won't take it."

When I congratulate Gerry on becoming the next owner of *China Cloud,* he shakes his head in bewilderment.

"I only came for advice on a new boat I planned to build. Of course I'd love to have *China Cloud,* but I've told Allen and Sharie to think very, very carefully before they come to a final decision about this."

When Allen returns in the dory after taking Gerry back to shore, he says to Sharie, "Honey, shall we ask him to take the cat as well?"

JUNE 5 ■ After a night of rain, a northwest wind chases away the clouds and reveals a freshly rinsed sky. With Allen and Sharie, we pick our way along the shore of Hope Bay, collecting fir bark to feed their stove.

"It dries out quickly, and it's got as much energy as coal," says Allen, handing me a piece.

The bark is coarsely textured, with deep furrows, and is a rich, marbled chestnut colour. We find chunks of it tangled up in wet, slippery seaweed, and wedged between rocks. Some have barnacles growing on them, others have been smoothed by waves. Only those the right size for the stove go into Allen's sack.

"Why do people cut down trees for fuel, when there's all this bark washed up on the beach?" he asks.

My hands have begun to itch from the tiny, almost invisible fibres that slough off the pieces of bark as I pick them up. I wonder about Sharie, whose skin is so delicate these days, so easily damaged.

"Oh, it never bothers me," she says, gazing at her hands. "I've been collecting bark off the beach for fifty years." She looks up at me and smiles. "I guess I must be tougher than I thought."

A truck pulls up above the beach. The small, elderly man who clambers down from it is dressed in jeans, sturdy boots, a red vest and a baseball cap. Nimbly, he hops across the rocks towards Allen and Sharie, who greet him enthusiastically.

"You look so well, Earl," they tell him.

Gerry Fossum hears some surprising news about China Cloud.

"I'm same as always," he says. "Healthy as a hog. Lots of things to keep me busy."

The Farrells first met Earl Hastings in the early sixties, when they were anchored at Browning Harbour on *Ocean Girl*. Allen needed some work done on his rudder, and Earl offered his services. He picked up the rudder late one evening and returned it early next morning, full of apologies about having taken so long.

"My dad always said that if you want something done, you should give it to a busy man," Allen chuckles.

Earl is just four years younger than Allen. Both men came of age during the Depression, and each emerged from those difficult years at opposite ends of a spectrum. In the early thirties Allen worked for a year as a rod man with the City of Vancouver surveying department. At the time about fifteen percent of the population of Vancouver were on unemployment or relief benefits, and work was near impossible to find. When Allen was fired from his job, he lived on the streets for a while and slept on benches. Finally he offered to work for free at the Cameron and Scott boat works, where he was given seventy-five cents a week for his tram car fare. He walked to work, and spent the money on food. When he married his first wife Betty in 1933, he was on relief. They lived in a room on Broadway, then moved out to Burrard Inlet, where settlements of squatters' cabins had grown up on the tidal flats. It was there he decided to build his first rowboat, escape the city and try fishing for a living.

First-hand experience of the injustices and indignities of the Depression years made Allen into a lifelong socialist. And it set him on a course of non-accumulation; he reasoned that the less he had, the less he could lose. Earl went the other way, establishing his own business and amassing land, houses, vehicles, an airfield and a plane.

"The secret of success is to do what you're good at," he tells us. "Look at Allen, the way he paints and builds beautiful boats. I couldn't do those things, no matter how hard I tried. But I'm good with metal, so I stuck with that. In 1934, I was in Victoria, and I wanted to be a machinist, but you couldn't buy a job in those days. I was building a twenty-seven-foot boat at the time, and I needed some work done on the propeller and the tail shaft, so I took it to a machine shop. Three weeks later I went back, and it wasn't done yet, but the owner, Mr. Watson, says to me, 'Just go ahead and do it yourself on our machines.' When he saw the work I did, he offered me a job. Well! I started the following Monday. I worked my way up, and I bought the place out in 1964."

Allen's socialist views are clear and simplistic, and usually he's suspicious about the motives of anyone who makes money. Earl, however, is an exception.

"You've never tried to get rich," he tells him. "You work harder than anyone I've ever met, but you're never too busy to help people. That's why things have always come your way."

Earl is still busy. As well as looking after his business interests, he cares for his wife, who is in poor health, and does all their cooking, shopping and housework. He tends a large garden, cans his own fruit and vegetables and makes preserves. He raises twenty-four beef cows and their calves. He mills wood for his neighbours and goes around mowing their fields and baling the hay. But he insists he has time to take me and Dag flying in his four-seater airplane.

"Come by in the morning and we'll see what the weather is doing," he says, fixing us with his bird-bright eyes. "We can't go up if it's too windy. My runway's really narrow, so I can't afford to make mistakes."

JUNE 6 ■ I see what Earl meant. The runway is a narrow strip, mown into a meadow of buttercups and high grasses. Earl built this airstrip himself.

"I was forty-three years old, I had a nice new home, and I needed a challenge. I said to myself, 'What can I do now? I can either become a millionaire or I can learn to fly.' So I got my ticket, and I got the plane, and then I had to have somewhere to go. I bought these twenty-six acres at a hundred dollars an acre, and I built myself this airstrip. I cut down trees, dug a pond eighteen feet deep in places for fill—oh, it was a really big job, I wouldn't do it now."

He points to the far side of the meadow, where bulrushes and snag trees emerge from a swamp.

"The beavers built a big dam in that pond. They're determined little critters, and as busy as me. If I broke through their dam right now, they'd have it fixed up by this afternoon."

As Earl gives us a quick tour around his airfield, it becomes obvious that he's a man who never gets rid of anything. At the back of the property are several sheds, housing a couple of small oil tank trucks, a sawmill, an array of farm machinery, and an assortment of old vehicles. The rust-eaten shell of a 1950s Prefect has been parked in the same place for so long it appears to have taken root, and is home to hundreds of spiders and their webs.

"I'm going to fix up that car," says Earl, looking at it appraisingly, "whenever I get time."

A path leads us past an earth-mover with thistles growing around it, and to the control tower. At the top of the tower is a narrow room, with floor to ceiling windows on two walls. A fridge, cookstove and bathroom fixtures lie around the floor, waiting to be installed.

"There's such a nice view from here," says Earl. "This place will double as a guest cabin, once I get around to finishing it."

To one side of the airstrip is a low silver hangar. Earl pushes open its sliding doors to reveal old fridges, stoves, washing machines, vacuum

Dag goes ashore by kayak in Hope Bay.

cleaners, sofas and garden furniture, piles of lumber, bags of fertilizer, coils of chicken wire, lengths of piping, several barnacle-encrusted out-board engines and, in the midst of all this, a bright red four-seater Stinson airplane.

"She was built in 1946," says Earl proudly. "She's nothing fancy, just the bare bones. The planes these days are full of expensive systems. It's because everyone's scared of getting sued for negligence. They even have a system to keep the windows clean, so that if you crash the passengers can't claim it was because the pilot couldn't see out properly."

I follow him around the plane as he does a preflight check. He slaps the struts, waggles the ailerons, kicks the tires. Finally, he lifts the engine cover and looks inside it.

Earl Hastings at the controls of his plane.

"Needs more oil," he pronounces. "There should be some in that drawer behind you."

The drawer is part of an old bedroom dressing table that's leaning against the wall. Rummaging through rusty nuts and bolts, I find a can of oil.

"Have you ever crashed?" I weakly ask him, as I hand it over.

"Only once," he says, unscrewing the cap. "Me and the wife were coming in to land at Qualicum and I mistook a fence for some long grass."

For a minute he concentrates on pouring the oil, while I consider the wisdom of going up in a plane that is almost fifty years old with a pilot who is close to eighty.

"I've got no insurance, by the way," he mentions casually, "so if anything goes wrong you're on your own."

Dag helps him to push the plane outside, and we all climb aboard. My hands have begun to sweat. Earl is so small that he can barely see over the engine cowling. He reaches for the only life jacket in sight, which is lying next to me on the back seat, and slips it under his rear end, raising himself up a good three inches. We taxi to the end of the runway, then sit for a few minutes while the engine warms up. I watch

Earl's wrinkled brown hand move across the control panel as he carefully checks each dial—oil, fuel, altimeter, oil pressure, temperature. Finally he slips on a pair of headphones, turns to me and smiles.

"Strapped in?"

The engine roars. We start to roll past tall grasses and buttercups, which look perilously close to the wheels. Then the grasses and flowers blur, and we're bumping along, like a big awkward bird trying to get off the ground. The road looms up, cars pass right in front of us and suddenly we're skimming over top of them. As the nose of the plane points skyward, Earl cranes his neck like a tortoise to see above the control panel. Pender Island drops away steadily until the boats in Browning and Bedwell harbours are tiny, and moored to matchstick docks. The subdivision around Magic Lake looks like a toy town, and over in Hope Bay miniaturized scale models of *China Cloud* and *Luna Moth* lie at anchor. We fly across Swanson Channel to Prevost Island, where specklike cows graze in fields that cut swathes through a forest. Spread out before us, the Gulf Islands are lush and lovely, with ferries threading between them across midnight-blue water, their white wakes trailing like bridal trains. For a few seconds I lose my fear—until I notice the daylight shining through a crack in the floor of the plane, right by one of the seat mountings. Grinning happily, Earl banks the plane steeply and points things out to Dag, who is snapping away with his camera. I stare wide-eyed through the crack, watching the blue of the ocean turn to the green of land as we return to Pender Island. The runway appears, a disconcertingly small slot in the forest. Earl dips the plane towards it, then suddenly pulls up again to avoid clipping the tops of some tall trees. I shut my eyes, and open them again too soon. Cars are right beneath the wheels of the plane and the landing strip is rising up to meet us. But we don't land exactly; we bound. Big, heart-stopping bounds that seem to go on for an eternity while I imagine a side wind catching us, the long grass tangling in a wheel, the plane spinning, flipping, exploding into flames . . . I cover my face with my hands and don't take them away until the engine has stopped and I can hear the buzz of crickets in the grass. We're parked right outside the hangar, and Earl is pulling off his headphones. He turns to me with a mischievous grin.

"Enjoy that?" he asks.

JUNE 7 ■ "We've been here long enough," says Allen over lunch. "It's time to go."

Around three o'clock, a light southerly breeze blows up and we take advantage of it to sail around into Clam Bay. Sharie steers the boat towards the shore of the bay while Allen throws the lead line overboard, carefully sounding before he drops his anchor. Behind a crescent gravel beach strewn with big silvery logs, there's an orchard of old gnarled trees surrounded by long grasses and wildflowers.

"What's the sign on that tree say?" asks Allen.

Through binoculars I scan the hand-scribed lettering: "PRIVATE PROPERTY. KEEP OUT."

"Oh no," says Allen, when I tell him. "It used to be a lovely place to go ashore. What's wrong with these people? Why don't they put up welcome signs?"

After dinner, we wander along the beach, peering at the remains of an old midden, admiring the sphagnum mosses growing from the trees, and the blue periwinkles spilling down the bank. Allen is as energetic as a puppy, skipping over logs and jogging up and down ahead of us.

"I've never liked running," Sharie tells me, as we walk arm-in-arm. "When we had sports days at school I was always last in the running races. But I usually won the egg and spoon race."

"That's because your balance was good from all the dancing you did," says Allen, jogging by.

Sharie has danced a lot during her life: as a child in Fort William to whatever her music teacher father played on the piano; as a teenager in Vancouver at the parties given by a German man, the owner of the dress shop where her mother worked, who expertly whirled her through polkas and tangos and waltzes; and as a young woman in amateur productions put on by Theatre Under The Stars in Vancouver's Stanley Park. Had she been given the chance, dancing may well have been her life. When she was small, a neighbour of her family who was a ballet teacher recognized her talent and offered her free lessons.

"My mother turned down the offer," Sharie recounts. "She said it would still be too expensive, what with the ballet shoes and clothes I'd need."

"Have you ever felt bitter about it?" I ask.

"Bitter?" She repeats the word as if it's from some foreign language she doesn't understand. "No, I've never felt that."

JUNE 8 ■ We're grateful to the two cheeky crows who wake us, hopping over our aft deck and pecking open the garbage bag I carelessly left exposed, because without them we might have missed the dawn. The sky is a palette of glorious colour, golden and pink and mauve and blue. Clam Bay is calm as a pond, but bustling with life. A fully grown bald eagle, its white head gleaming, swoops down with talons outstretched and grabs a fish from just beneath the surface. Close by an otter swims about, also fishing for its breakfast. Every few minutes it dives, popping up a little later and noisily chomping on its catch. Sometimes it floats on its back to eat, with the end of its fat tail sticking out of the water.

By six o'clock the eagle has retreated to the trees and the otter has swum to shore and disappeared behind a log. In their place is a kingfisher. It hovers over the water, then drops into it like a stone, time and time again. I watch it, mesmerized, until Dag says quietly, "The beach." A deer and two fawns have appeared from the trees. For a minute the mother stands motionless while her spotted offspring vigorously nose her teats and begin to suck. Then she lifts her head, sniffs the air and pulls away. The fawns scamper after her as she disappears into the cover of the woods. I clamber down the rudder post for a swim. The water is so clear I can see ten feet to the bottom, where a large red rock crab scuttles along, raising clouds of mud.

Allen appears on the deck of *China Cloud,* gazing about. In Navy Channel, logs float by towards the south, pulled by the current. There's a light southerly wind, but puffy clouds are starting to move from the northwest, trailing long wisps behind them. He hangs a cloth weighted with lead over the skylight of the main cabin—a sign that he's going to do some painting, and we won't be going anywhere this morning.

JUNE 9 ■ By seven o'clock we're on our way across Swanson Channel, going with the ebb tide and a favourable breeze towards Prevost. The island is owned by descendants of Hubert de Burgh, a thirteenth-century English baron who was one of the guardians appointed to ensure the maintenance of the Magna Carta, the great charter of English civil liberties. Last night I asked Allen if he'd ever been to Prevost.

"Oh, yes," he'd chuckled. "I was there when old Digby de Burgh was getting the farm going."

Digby Hussey de Burgh was originally from Limerick, Ireland. In 1926 he and his son Hubert started clearing land on Prevost for seed pasture and to keep sheep, cattle and goats. In 1930 he hired a logging outfit from Vancouver to come in and take down trees. It was a new operation owned by several people, including a preacher and the father of Allen's best friend, Len. Allen, eighteen years old and eager for work, told Len's father that he already had a little logging experience. Five years before, he'd spent a summer working on his father's horse-logging show in the Fraser Valley. His job then had been to walk along in front of the horses with a tin can full of old motor oil and a rag, greasing the skids the logs ran along. Now he found himself loading a tractor, a boomer and a pile of shiplap onto a scow, which was then towed by tug from Vancouver, across the strait and through Active Pass.

"We were in the middle of the pass, I was sitting on the bow of the tug and Len was on the tow bit. The water was running fast and swirling about, so I called Len to come and see. Just as he jumped off, the tow bit broke and the scow broke loose. He would have been killed by the cable whipping back if I hadn't called him. We managed to get the scow ashore, and made another tow bit out of the trunk of a yew tree. Then we carried on to Prevost Island, cleared some land, built some bunkhouses and started logging. I was the chokerman—I attached the logs to the tractor and followed them down to the water. Old de Burgh said to us, 'Clear every tree! I want this place to look like Ireland!' "

Luckily, that didn't happen. It turned out that no one in the logging show was very experienced, and it folded within a couple of months.

"When they dropped me off in Vancouver, all the wages I had was a pair of new boots," laughs Allen, "and the ten pounds I'd gained because of all the food I'd eaten."

By eight we're skirting the southern end of Prevost, going with the current. After rounding the point protecting Ellen Bay, we head up Captain Passage. Changing course again, we start crossing the channel between Prevost and Saltspring islands. Here, wind and current are working against each other, producing a steep chop. As we plough into the waves our boats slow perceptibly and the wind seems to gust even harder. Our tentative plan is to check out the anchorage in Annette Inlet on the northwest side of the island. Its entrance is narrow, bounded by steep bluffs and peppered with rocks. Dag sails into it against the wind and current, coming perilously close to the bluffs each time before changing tack. Behind us, Allen has hove to, and is obviously waiting for us to return.

"If *China Cloud* isn't coming, why are we going in?" I ask Dag.

"Because it's great practice," he answers cheerfully.

Once we're through, he turns the boat and we fly back out.

"I was thinking of having a go, but it looked like an awful, exposed place to anchor in there," calls Allen. "What's the point of a battle with no reward at the end?"

With a fair wind and a following sea, we sail over Trincomali Channel to Retreat Cove on Galiano Island.

"This isn't a good place to anchor either," says Allen. "If a qualicum blows up we'll be in trouble."

Qualicums are strong westerly or southwesterly winds which blow up suddenly, usually after the passage of a front. They are named after the place on Vancouver Island where they are particularly strong. From the Pacific Ocean, they funnel through the Alberni Inlet and a gap in the mountains, then spill over Qualicum Beach and into the Strait of Georgia.

"We won't stay here longer than one night," Allen decides.

When he and Sharie last anchored here in the fifties, they met a man called Robin Ridington, who was on a small boat tied up close to them. Now Robin and his second wife own the steep, rocky island in Retreat Cove. At one end of it is a tiny bay with a small, crushed-shell beach. Above it, on a mossy knoll, a wooden sign is tacked onto an arbutus tree. "On August 10 1992," it reads, "Jillian and Robin Ridington commenced stewardship of Retreat Island." At the other end of the island is a dock with more signs: "STOP!" "PRIVATE ISLAND," "NO TRESPASSING," "BEWARE OF THE DOG."

Two very mellow dogs greet us on the dock. We follow them up a steep path to a beautiful new guest house and a studio in the finishing stage of construction, where Robin and Jillian are deep in discussion with a construction crew. They are delighted to see the Farrells, and invite us all to their main house for a drink. The house is large and spacious, built on several levels, with expansive ocean vistas. We sit outside, on a deck high above the water, where Jillian serves us with cranberry juice and cookies. Allen seems rather cranky—he grumbles about the ice in his drink, fishes it out and flings it over his shoulder.

"I'm fed up with sailing," he tells Robin. "We're giving away the boat and going to Mexico. We'll live on the beach and I'll build a little dory."

Robin smiles sagely. "Twenty years ago, Allen, when you were living in the float house on Lasqueti Island and building *August Moon,* you told me, 'That's it, no more boats, only this little dory.' "

"Did I? Well, that was twenty years ago. This time I mean it."

On the way back to our boats, he is silent, except to comment that the clouds are moving in from a different direction.

"A mackerel sky, not twenty-four hours dry," he says, quoting an old proverb.

On *China Cloud,* Dag and I prepare a supper of scrambled eggs, bacon, onions, a can of sockeye salmon and a salad of the fresh greens that Jillian picked for us from her garden.

"I'm depressed," Allen announces, halfway through the meal. "I don't understand why people need so much. When I was a kid I used to visit a friend who lived in a great big house, with twenty rooms, and I always got depressed there, too."

Sharie reads his mind, and lays a hand on his knee.

"Honey, that house we were in today is beautiful."

"Sure it is. But do you remember Ted's place on Ruxton Island? It was a one-room cabin, and he'd built every stick of it himself. I wasn't depressed there."

"It's hard for people to resist the urge to accumulate things," Dag tells him. "You're very unusual that way, you know."

Allen fixes him with a level gaze. "Am I? I just don't understand that. I'm glad we're giving everything away."

Back on *Luna Moth,* Dag and I talk late into the night about how simply the Farrells live, how purely they follow a philosophy of non-attachment to material possessions, how little they take from the planet. We count up the things we've accumulated: land, a house filled with appliances, a car, bicycles, kayaks, this sailboat. In vain, we try to imagine giving everything away and moving on without a backward glance, as Allen and Sharie are soon about to do.

JUNE 10 ■ In the night a westerly wind blows up, whistling through the cove and forcing us to move *Luna Moth* towards the protection of the dock. The water is full of phosphorescent plankton. As Dag yulohs, I watch the long glittering shapes of fish shooting through the water. When I drop the anchor there's an explosion of light, and the chain is transformed into a thick rope of sparkling silver. Soon after we crawl back into our sleeping bag, rain starts hammering down and our canopy flaps and billows. Around six, the wind and rain ease off. We fall into a deep sleep until, at eight, we're woken by *China Cloud*'s bell, and Allen's call.

"Are you guys ready to go?"

The sky and sea are a flat grey. Soon a steady drizzle sets in. Wispy clouds, like vapours, hang in the trees along the cliffs of Galiano Island. It's strangely quiet in the channel. Only occasionally do we hear the drone of a distant outboard engine, the wild cry of a solitary loon, the snort of a seal. Ahead of us, *China Cloud* moves silently through the mist. On our boat, all is quiet save for the sound of water along the hull, and the rustling of Dag's rain jacket as he pulls in the sheet.

"I'm learning a hell of a lot from sailing without an engine," he says suddenly.

I turn to look at him. He's sitting at the tiller, with rain dripping from the sou'wester pulled down over his eyes.

"It's all about accepting the weather," he continues, "and how the wind and waves move the boat. You have to go with the elements rather than fighting them. It's no good pushing and striving to get somewhere. You have to allow things to happen, and know when to take a chance. But you need to take your time, and hardly anyone is willing to do that."

"It sounds as if you're learning about more than sailing," I say.

He nods. "I'm beginning to understand what it means to be in tune with the sea and the land. Take Allen and Sharie—maybe they have such a deep bond with their environment because they're so dependent on it. They've relied on the natural things around them to build boats and shelters. They've used simple tools and done everything by hand. But it's never been a hardship for them—they've survived with a flourish, with elegance. And they've left no damage in their wake."

Just before three o'clock we reach the south end of False Narrows with a breeze behind us. I lean over the side of the boat to look at the fronds of bull kelp floating in the water. They're being pushed north-wards; the current is still with us. As we're passing the reef, the fronds go limp, and hang downwards. Within minutes, as the tide switches, they rise back to the surface and ripple southwards. Dag starts furiously yulohing, the light breeze stays with us and somehow we squeak through. *China Cloud* is heading towards Jack Point, catching the good southeaster blowing up the channel, and soon she has receded to a dot on the horizon.

■

In the evening, we leave *Luna Moth* anchored close to *China Cloud* and go to check on our house. The place seems so big, so opulent. I walk around, touching the windows, the humming fridge, the kitchen counters and the pictures on the walls, wondering at the unfamiliarity of it all. And when I sit down at the table, the ground rocks beneath my feet.

CHAPTER FOUR

North to Lasqueti Island

JUNE 11-15 ■ The house, and life ashore, reclaim us for a while. Allen and Sharie are busy with visitors, and with doctor and dentist appointments in Nanaimo, but on several occasions they row over to have dinner with us and do their laundry.

"When shall we come?" they ask. They are always scrupulously punctual; five minutes before the appointed time they row around the reef between Newcastle and Protection islands, and on the dot of the hour the bow of their dory scrapes the beach in front of our house.

Even on warm evenings, we crank up the electric heating, and they slide into their usual place, on a bench right above a baseboard heater.

"Ahhhh," sighs Allen happily, as he feels the draft of warm air on his back. "I can't wait to get to Mexico."

Dag cooks them dinners of roast pork, and I make desserts slathered in whipped cream. Allen refuses to eat white flour, sugar or processed food, and drinks only water and the occasional herb tea, but he loves his fat.

"They used to call me Ham Fat Farrell in Bargain Harbour," he says, accepting more pork crackling from Dag and putting lots of butter on his potatoes.

He gets cross with Sharie for bringing their laundry. Usually they do it on the boat, by hand. Sometimes, Allen fills the bathtub with rainwater he heats on the stove, and then treads the washing with his feet.

"A washing machine is the one thing I would have liked," Sharie confides, as we take sheets from the dryer and fold them.

In her fifty years with Allen, she has done without the conveniences most North American women take for granted—running water, flush toilets, electric light and heat. When they met in 1945, she had a secretarial job in downtown Vancouver, fashionable clothes, a group of artistic friends. Leaving all this behind, she moved into Allen's cabin at Bargain Harbour, near Pender Harbour, and started planning to build a boat with him and sail away to the South Seas.

"You gave up a lot for that man of yours," I tease her.

"I don't regret any of it," she says seriously. "Except for the washing machine."

JUNE 16 ■ A strong high-pressure system is building over the coast. We move back onto *Luna Moth* and anchor next to *China Cloud* in Newcastle Island's Echo Bay. Allen and Sharie welcome us warmly, as if we've just returned home from another country. While we're having afternoon tea with them, I worry aloud that I might have forgotten to lock the back door of the house.

"We never lock the boat," Sharie tells me. "We don't have any keys. We used to have one for our mailbox on Lasqueti, but we threw it away."

JUNE 17 ■ In Thrifty's supermarket, where we're provisioning for the next part of our trip, Allen seems out of his depth. Clutching the shopping cart like a protective shield, he sets off along an aisle, ducking his head and shifting his gaze from side to side, as if he's fearful of snipers hiding among the cereal cartons. Sharie, who is clinging to his arm, keeps pleading with him to stop so that she can take what she needs from the shelves.

"Wait, honey, we need soya milk. And cheese—be patient, honey, until I choose some."

But Allen is not a patient man.

"God, this air-conditioning is awful, I'm *freezing*," he complains, hugging himself and squinting against the bright lights. "Why would anyone want to come in here and be cold?"

On the way back across the harbour, Sharie tells me about shopping in Nanaimo in the forties. She and Allen used to tie up in *Wind Song* at Farmers' Landing, at the site of today's fisherman's wharf, where farmers from Gabriola off-loaded their produce. Above it was Stannard's Feed Store and Schwartz's Photography and behind it, where now there are roads, buildings and a bus parkade, a lagoon stretched to Commercial and Wharf streets.

"We could row right up to the shops. But there was never much to choose from. Nanaimo had the reputation of being hopeless for shopping. Mostly we used to order what we needed from Vancouver, and it would be delivered on the Union Steamships."

"We'd make a list of everything we needed," Allen adds. "Anchors, engines, a thousand feet of lumber, a case of milk, a couple of cabbages. We put the list in an envelope and mailed it off. The next week the steamer would come from Vancouver, with all our stuff on it. Oh, those steamships were lovely. They were big and luxurious, with red carpets everywhere. At dinner time someone would be playing the piano and there'd be linen tablecloths and silver and a hunk of butter in a dish. And three-course meals—*real* food. What do you get now on the ferry? Plastic food wrapped in plastic. And you sit on plastic seats. In those days you sat on soft plush seats. Everybody used the steamer. Old loggers and miners sitting on all this plush stuff, talking big talk about how many millions they were going to make."

From the deck of *China Cloud,* we can see through the gap between Protection and Newcastle islands and out into the strait. A B.C. ferry steams by, on its way towards Departure Bay. The wind brings the beat of its engines, and the tinny sound of a message being played on its public address system.

"Everyone looked forward to the steamships coming," says Sharie. "They linked all the small coastal communities. It was so sad when they stopped running."

JUNE 18 ■ We row over to Newcastle Island for a walk and to collect pine needles for Mario's litter. The Newcastle ferry has just arrived and is off-loading throngs of tourists. This island has a long tradition as a recreational area. In 1890, the Vancouver Coal Company

Nanaimo Harbour from Echo Bay, Newcastle Island.

created the first picnic grounds. Forty-one years later, the CPR established the Newcastle Island Resort. Steamships brought excursionists from Vancouver and Bellingham to enjoy the resort's pool, playing fields and riding stables, and the dances in its pavilion. As well as leisure activities, however, the island also had industry. Coal was mined here from 1850, when there are records of British gunboats calling in for fuel, until 1903. A sandstone quarry was established in 1869, originally to supply stone to the contractors building the Federal Mint in San Francisco. And there were thriving Japanese herring salteries until 1942, when the Japanese were forced to leave the coast. Long before all of this, there was a Coast Salish winter village, Saysetsen, where people are now playing Frisbee and throwing sticks for their dogs.

A path above the beach takes us to Kanaka Bay, on the north side of the island. Kanakas were the Hawaiians, or Sandwich Islanders, who emigrated to British Columbia during the nineteenth century. One of them, Peter Kakua, murdered his Coast Salish wife, baby and mother-in-law along with the man he found them all in bed with. For this crime he was hanged on Gallows Point at the south end of Protection Island, then buried close to Kanaka Bay.

"Imagine murdering someone just because he's in bed with your wife," says Allen thoughtfully. "I mean, that guy was only doing what comes naturally. It's all because of our gonads."

On the way back we take a route through the forest, filling a plastic bag with pine needles as we go. Sharie gamely toils up a steep part of the path, holding onto Allen with one hand and a stout stick with the other.

"Do you remember when we walked here with your mum and had to pull her up this path?" Allen asks her. "I don't have to do that for you now, and you're eight years older than she was then!"

Just before we reach the dock, he flips himself forward and starts walking across the grass on his hands. Some tourists on their way to the ferry gape at him in astonishment.

"Look at that old man doing tricks!" a little boy cries to his mother.

"Can't go as far as I once could," grumbles Allen, flipping back onto his feet, his face bright red. "I'm not as strong as I used to be."

JUNE 19 ■ Allen thinks that in the next couple of days the winds will switch from northwesterlies to southerlies, and blow us to our next planned stop of Wallis Point, in Nanoose Bay. Known locally as Powder Point, this used to be the site of an ammunition factory, which blew up around 1920. At high tides, the end of the point becomes an island. In 1937 Allen built a shack and lived there with his first wife, Betty, and their two young sons from the fall until the following spring, trying to make a living from fishing.

"It was a cold, hard, hungry winter," he says ruefully. "There were no fish. I had no raingear except for gumboots, and I lost those. I was out in the rowboat when a cresting wave capsized it. Then more waves came and rolled it several times. I had to kick off the boots so I could swim and get the oars and string seat."

In desperation, he asked for Relief, only to be told he hadn't lived in the area long enough to be eligible for it. Instead, however, he was offered a road-building job near Nanoose.

"Every morning I'd row over the harbour to go to work. It was packed with sea lions back then, and the government boats would be out there shooting them with machine guns. Sometimes the bullets would ricochet and barely miss our cabin. I'd come back to find bullet shells in the boat, or sometimes the native Indians would have borrowed it to go hunting—but they always returned it. I'd buy spuds for one cent a pound and carrots for three cents a pound from a farmer in Nanoose, and row home with a hundredweight sack of each in the boat."

Despite the hardships of that winter, Allen still found time to dream. He put up a boat shed on Powder Point, and as well as building a double-ended rowboat, he started laying a keel for a sailboat that could take him to the South Seas. But when spring came, he and his family left to go fishing. It was a year before they returned to the point; by then the cabin and the shed had fallen down, and someone had sawn up the keel for firewood.

JUNE 20 ■ Still the northwester blows. Allen stands on deck, reading the thermometer.

"The air is seventy-four degrees, the water's sixty-five," he calls to us. "Brrr! Still too cold."

He spends the morning scraping the cabin top, getting it ready for a fresh coat of paint. In the old days he used to make his own paint with white lead and linseed oil, adding things like lamp black for colour. As it's not possible to buy white lead these days, he has to be content with mixing his own colours from manufactured paints to get the tones he wants. I comment on the muted colours of the cabin top and sides, and the warm reddish shade, reminiscent of lacquer ware, lining the dory.

"I call that Chinese red," says Allen. "You mix red, orange and black. It's easy to do."

In the afternoon Ivan Bulic, an old friend of the Farrells, comes by to tell us about a peaceful demonstration planned on the open day of the Canadian Forces Maritime Experimental and Test Ranges base, in Nanoose Bay. This facility, which is used by the U.S. and Canadian navies, encompasses the shores of the bay and some of the surrounding islands, and also includes Area WG. Known as Whiskey Golf, after the International Radio transmission names for call letters, this five- by fifteen-mile area of the Strait of Georgia is used for the testing of underwater weapons. Whenever Whiskey Golf is active, which is usually

Danny Norrie

In light breezes, Luna Moth *is able to keep up with* China Cloud.

five days of the week, boats are banned from entering it. On principle, the Farrells refuse to acknowledge the ban. Six months ago, they sailed with Dag from Nanaimo to Lasqueti Island, passing through Whiskey Golf when it was active. A military plane harassed them, flying low over *China Cloud* and buzzing it several times. Now, Ivan tells us that Wallis Point is part of the base, and that we won't be allowed to anchor or go ashore there to see where Allen had his old cabin. For Allen, a confirmed pacifist, the irony of this is hard to bear.

"But it was our home!" he cries unhappily. "How can they do that? I'm never going anywhere near there again. And we're too old now to demonstrate. They'd just come alongside in their ugly steel boats and arrest us."

J U N E 2 1 ■ Around three o'clock, while we're having afternoon tea on *China Cloud,* the wind switches, and starts blowing from the southeast. After a brief discussion we agree to sail up to Ballenas Islands for the night, with me aboard *China Cloud.* While Allen pulls up the anchor I help Sharie hoist the mainsail. She goes below to clear away dishes, and I sit next to Allen, leaning against the stanchion. Skilfully, he tacks between all the boats anchored in the harbour. As we come about in the narrow gap between Newcastle and Protection islands, all three sails swing from port to starboard, and set on a port tack without Allen touching a line.

"The boat sails herself," he says. "I just sit here and push the tiller. When I built her, I didn't know if she was going to work. Instead of having one keel I put two on the sides—you call them bilge keels. That way I could let her go high and dry. I said to Sharie, 'Honey, if she does-n't work well at least we can just put her up on the beach and live aboard.' And then we got her in the water and we were really happy with how she sailed. I can do almost everything from the cockpit. And if I want to reef down, I call to my eighty-eight-year-old wife and she lets go the halyard and there the sail's reefed, no problem. And see the rake of the foremast? I made it like that because that's what I saw in pic-tures. But when I go wing and wing . . ." He notices my blank expres-sion. "Wing and wing is when I run with the wind and the foresail is on one side of the mast and the mainsail on the other. Well, when that happens, the foresail automatically sets on one side and stays there. I don't have to do anything, it's so easy. You won't read about that in any theory books on sailing. Some scientists say that in theory bumblebees can't fly. Don't ever believe scientists and theories."

For the first time, I've noticed how small the tiller is—only three feet in length, and made from a narrow piece of yew.

"It doesn't need to be any bigger," Allen explains, "because the rud-der is balanced. That means some of its area is ahead of the rudder post, so there's less strain on the tiller."

Framed by the gap is Snake Island, a windswept scrap of land out in the strait. Dag and I often kayak there, but Allen has only ever sailed past it.

"Does it have snakes?" he asks me.

I tell him that we once saw a very large garter snake on the island, but that according to a legend recorded by the Coast Salish, many more live there. It's said that one springtime a young woman was in Departure Bay, collecting new shoots to eat, and that some of the plants were cov-ered with white foam. Within a few months her stomach began to swell and it was soon obvious she was pregnant. Refusing to listen to her protestations of innocence, her father banished her to a small island. After a while her mother grew worried for her daughter and went out to the island in a dugout. As she drew near she saw her daughter standing on the shore, surrounded by snakes. The white foam her daughter had eaten months before contained the eggs of snakes, and she had given birth to hundreds of them.

By four o'clock we're passing Five Fingers Islands. The sun is warm, and *China Cloud* is cruising happily along in a steady ten-knot wind, creaking like a basket. Sharie joins us in the cockpit, bringing cushions for us all to sit on. It's comfortable enough without them; like elsewhere on the boat there are no sharp corners up here, only curved, smooth wood.

"The wind's too good to stop," says Allen. "We could make it up to Lasqueti Island, right into False Bay."

"Aren't we going to Ballenas, honey?" asks Sharie. "I don't want to be travelling in the dark. And what if the wind drops? Let's find a safe anchorage soon."

We slip by Piper's Lagoon where, on Shack Islands, a group of old fishermen's shacks still stand, looking as they did fifty years ago.

"In the Depression," says Allen, "a lot of people came up along the coast on rowboats, trying to make a living. They'd see the salmon, and they'd see a packer picking the fish up, and they'd think, oh, I guess I'll go and live there. They'd go and find some driftwood on the beach and make themselves a little shack and they'd fish. Nothing organized, it just happened."

During the blueback runs in mid-May, there would be up to five hundred rowboats working between Nanaimo and the northern end of Lasqueti Island. Many of the fishermen had built their own boats and had simple gear—green cotton line, half-pound leads, hooks, herring rakes and spinners. They kept close to the packers, who often advanced them food and tobacco. It was Jim Warburton, a friend of his father's, who in 1934 suggested Allen should build a rowboat and join these roving fishermen. When it was finished he and Betty got a tow up the coast to Smuggler Cove, then to Lasqueti Island, where they moved into an empty shack in Squitty Bay.

Allen and Betty's cabin on Squitty Bay, Lasqueti Island, 1934.

"We were really free, because we had so little," says Allen nostalgi-cally. "Just the boat, some blankets, a tarp, cooking pots and a few tools. We stayed there all that summer. Over on Sangster Island there were lots of cabins, and sometimes there'd be forty rowboats all out fishing together. We got about ten cents a fish if we were lucky—we made no money, but we had a good time."

At the summer's end they returned to Lynnmour, in North Vancouver. Allen got a job in the mill and took gym classes. In 1936 he won the B.C. championship for gymnastics and tumbling, and landed a job as a gym instructor in Chilliwack. Teaching came naturally to him, but he missed the coast terribly. So, in the back room of his lodgings he started building a couple of twelve-foot sailboats. When the spring of 1937 came around he gave up his job, and with Betty and their two baby sons set off down the Fraser River.

"We put the babies in apple boxes and took one box in each boat. It was freshet season and the river was running fast, so it was pretty exciting. At Steveston we could smell the salt air—ah, it was so lovely.

We rowed and sailed up the coast, and at night we slept on blankets on the beach and cooked clams over a fire. We fished again that summer round Lasqueti Island, then came down here to Nanoose Bay for the winter fishing."

Through the sliding window, Sharie passes out a mug of hot water for Allen, and tea for herself and me. A plate of cheese and crackers follows.

"Honey, shouldn't we stop for the night at Ballenas, after all?" she asks Allen. "It will soon be dark and cold."

He doesn't answer. He's staring at the Winchelsea Islands, once a part of his old fishing grounds, now part of the Nanoose Base and installed with facilities to track underwater weapons.

"Bombs," he mutters darkly. "War. It's what keeps the system going."

He goes below, leaving me and Sharie at the tiller. We sit in companionable silence until *Luna Moth* draws alongside us. Dag is lying on the edge of the cockpit, looking perfectly relaxed.

"Shouldn't we start steering in towards Ballenas?" he calls.

"I think Allen wants to get to False Bay," Sharie tells him.

He sits up. "Lasqueti, tonight? It's already six o'clock."

Allen's head appears in the hatchway. "What do you want to do, Dag?"

Dag pauses, looking faintly irritated.

"I thought we were heading to Ballenas. What do you want to do, Allen?"

"I don't mind."

"Honey, let's not end up drifting about in the dark," Sharie pleads.

Allen scratches his beard. "We might have westerlies tomorrow. Then we'd be stuck. Maybe we should head for False Bay."

Sharie turns to me with a wry smile. "He always gets his way."

As the sun sets, I'm alone at the tiller while Allen and Sharie eat supper below. Sangster Island slips by to our starboard, the snowcapped peaks of Forbidden Plateau to our port. Ahead, *Luna Moth* is silhouetted against a vivid pink sky, and a gleam of golden light from one of the last of the sun's rays shines through a frayed part of the sail. By the time we're passing Jenkins Island, darkness is closing in, and the wind is dropping.

"What speed are we doing?" I ask Allen, when he joins me in the cockpit.

"About the same as a slow walk." He sighs heavily. "I'm too old for this boat business. It's all right when you're young, about sixty or seventy. But not now. I'd rather go somewhere warm, and paint."

It's almost midnight before we turn into False Bay, and finally drop anchor.

"Sharie really wanted to stop earlier in the day," I tell Dag, when we're in bed together. "Allen wouldn't listen to her, yet she wasn't in the least bit cross. If you'd done that to me, I'd have been spitting nails."

"Well, she's had fifty years to get to know him," says Dag. "And they balance each other. She's the rock; he's the compulsive dreamer. Her strength allows him to follow his dreams, and he's given her the adventurous life she always wanted."

He pauses, then adds teasingly, "A good model for us, eh?"

JUNE 22   ■   False Bay is infamous for the Qualicum winds that blow into it with little or no warning, sometimes reaching storm force. For safety, *China Cloud* is tucked away at the end of a protected lagoon, at the southeast end of the bay. Allen and Sharie have just rowed over to shore and are heading up the path towards the post office. Dwarfed by tall trees, brightly dressed and hand in hand, from a distance they look much as they do in photographs circa 1971, when they bought land here on Lasqueti.

From the latter part of the nineteenth century, when the first white settlers arrived, until the 1930s, the population of Lasqueti never reached more than around a hundred. During the Depression years it tripled, as unemployed workers like Allen came here to farm, fish and forage. Although many left during and after the Second World War, the population was kept buoyant by a logging boom that started in the late forties and lasted for a decade. After the boom ended, the population dwindled to less than fifty people, and by some accounts at one time dropped to seventeen.

A new era began in the sixties when young people, some of them draft-dodgers from the United States, came here to try living from the land. They squatted, beachcombed for building materials and grew their own food. Unlike the temporary settlers of the Depression years, they were doing this by choice rather than necessity, seeking an alternative

Allen Farrell collection

Sharie working on the new house, Lasqueti Island, 1971.

to the materialistic world they'd grown up in. When the Farrells bought their land in 1971 they were fifty-nine and sixty-four, the oldest hippies of all.

It was Allen's son Keray who told them about a five-acre lot for sale, a mile from the beach. Allen was rather fed up with sailing at the time, so he decided to go ashore. He built a house they could share with Sharie's mother and Keray's family, and he sold *Native Girl*, the boat he and Sharie had lived on since 1965.

"But we were all miserable," he told us this morning. "Sharie's mum was lonely for her friends in Vancouver. Keray split up from his wife so he was depressed. I was so sad that I'd sold *Native Girl*, and Sharie and I hated living in the woods. We woke up every morning with a big black cloud over us. Then Keray went to live in a cabin on Wolf Island in False Bay. We were visiting him one time, and we were on the beach collecting bark, and it was so wonderful to be back by the water. So we thought, we'll give the place in the woods to Keray and we'll build a float house in False Bay."

Within weeks, the house was built from beachcombed materials.

"It was a cosy place, all covered in shakes. For our stove we got a box full of gravel, the top third of an oil drum with a hinged door cut in it and a hole for the stove pipe to go through. To make bread or pies we set the pans on a grating on top of the stove and put the dishpan over it."

It wasn't too long, however, before the Farrells were fully afloat again. In September 1975 they launched *August Moon,* a twenty-seven-foot dory. By the following spring they had sold her, bought back *Native Girl* and moved aboard.

Not surprisingly, Lasqueti Island remained their base, for it was, and still is, a place where it is possible to live simply and in harmony with nature. A strong sense of community prevails, and over the years its residents have resolutely fought off the development ravaging other Gulf Islands. Thanks to their efforts the island has no car ferry, no hydroelectricity, no marinas.

But even on Lasqueti, holding back the tide of change is a never-ending process. The Farrells return from the post office looking distressed. Someone they met on the way told them that a few islanders are now pushing to ban people living in boats or float houses along the shores of Lasqueti.

"They're talking about people like us!" cries Allen, shaking his head in dismay. "What's the world coming to?"

JUNE 23 ■ We sail *Luna Moth* across False Bay to visit friends on Wolf Island. Misha, the Samoyed in residence, does a passable wolf impersonation as we drop anchor close to the shore, throwing back its head and howling to announce our arrival.

For decades Wolf Island was inhabited from time to time by squatters and seasonal fishermen and clam diggers. When Don Dempster and Judy Batstone bought it in 1979, they were living and working abroad and a man called Lorrie was squatting in a tiny cabin at its northern end. In time, Don and Judy returned to Canada, Lorrie moved across to Lasqueti and they bought his cabin and made it their home. Don, a civil engineer for the petroleum industry, conducts much of his business from its loft via cellular phone, computer and modem, which he powers by windmill-generated electricity.

Wolf Island may now be part of the information highway, but its plumbing arrangements are still very basic. Misha pads in front of me along a path through the woods to the guest outhouse. An old rowboat is turned over and propped up at one end to shelter a wooden toilet seat, set in a frame over a deep pit. Lifting the lid of the seat, I disturb a couple of large spiders busily reconstructing the webs ruined by the last visitors. When I've finished here, the dog leads me to the shower, which hangs from a peeling arbutus tree. Thanks to Don's water-heating system —black piping left lying on a rock where it will get maximum sun—I have a luxuriously warm shower that soaks the salt from my skin.

Judy has painstakingly created a vegetable garden in various nooks and crannies around this rocky, seven-acre island, and in miniature greenhouses made by stretching plastic over wooden frames. We return to the Farrells with her gifts of artichokes, hot peppers, zucchini, two types of lettuce and a bouquet of fresh herbs—lovage, basil, dill, fennel, cilantro. While we've been away, other islanders have visited *China Cloud,* bringing freshly picked raspberries, tender young green beans, homemade cookies.

"We often come back to the boat and find fruit and vegetables left on deck," says Sharie. "People here are so kind to us."

At half past three we sail out of False Bay and anchor close to the Finnerties, a handful of rocky, uninhabited islets. As he rows us over to them, Allen points to a beach facing south and strewn with driftwood.

"That's where most of *China Cloud* came from," he says. "We used to come over here in *Native Girl,* collect wood and tow it back to Scottie Bay."

In a narrow channel between two of the islets we gaze up at wind-flattened juniper trees growing from the steep bluffs, and the stonecrop and yellow gumweed blooming above them. Allen turns into a small lagoon and we go ashore. Over a century ago, the native Pentlatch people used to come here to forage for food and dig for clams. Allen followed suit, first with Betty in the thirties and later with Sharie.

"June was my favourite month here," he says. "There were fish and clams all year, but in June you could get a real variety of food."

He and Sharie point out the edible plants: the narrow fleshy leaves of goose tongue or sea plantain; sea asparagus, which they call chicken

Allen and Sharie show Maria the wild plants that used to be a staple of their diet.

claws; nodding onions that have just finished blooming; wild beach peas with fat little pods that are just starting to green up.

"Try these," says Allen, opening a pod and tipping the peas into my hand. "They're nice and sweet now. Later in the year I used to dry them and grind them into meal."

Just above the beach, prickly pear cacti are growing in mats along the ground. The Farrells roasted these to remove the prickles, then ate the flesh inside. They dug up and boiled the bulbs of the camas plant, part of the lily family. And they collected all kinds of seaweed, including bull kelp.

"We soaked the bulbs in two lots of fresh water, then sliced them and put them in a brine of vinegar, salt, water and herbs," Sharie tells me. "If you get them early enough in the season they're lovely and crunchy. And I dried the fronds and used them in soups."

Sometimes, Allen ate termites.

"They're nice if you pull off the heads. Once I was sitting eating them and my little granddaughter Kari-Ann said, 'What's that Grandpa? Can I have some?' I said, 'Sure you can, but only a couple because they're very special.' Because they were special she loved them and wanted more. Then her mother found out and told her that termites were bad. She wouldn't touch them after that."

Before we get back into the dory I pick chicken claws, goose tongue and pea pods. When I ask Sharie if she'd like me to cook some up for her at suppertime, she shakes her head.

"No thanks. I've eaten enough of them in the past. The taste is too strong for me now. I'll stick to our green beans."

Tucked away deep in the woods on one of the Finnerty Islands is a tiny one-roomed cabin, with a wood stove in the middle of the floor and sleeping benches along the walls. In the thirties this was the home of Pete Dubois. He took his fish packer around Lasqueti, north to Denman and Hornby islands, and as far south as the Winchelsea Islands, collecting fish from people like Allen, and selling it to the big packer boats which transported it to Vancouver.

"He lived here with his wife and six lovely daughters," says Allen.

"Eight of them, in this cabin?" I say, astonished.

"That's how it was in those days. People didn't worry about space and privacy like they do now. Over on the Fegans, there'd be all these cabins close together and someone new would arrive and the people would say, 'There's twelve feet between these two shacks, you can build a place here.'"

We sail on, towards the Fegan Islands. The sun is dipping down in the sky, casting a golden glow over the snowfields of Mount Arrowsmith. A couple of seals frolic about, slapping their tails hard on the flat, calm water. The wind dies off, and soon there is barely a ripple on the water.

"What kind of engine are you using, Farrell?" calls Dag, as *China Cloud* glides by us.

"It's called willpower," comes the answer.

By eight o'clock both Dag and Allen have resorted to their yulohs, and it's almost ten before we finally reach the Fegans. As soon as Allen prepares to anchor, we get a puff of wind.

"That's a docking breeze," says Allen, as we raft up to *China Cloud*. "We always get one just as we're dropping the hook."

Before we say good night, Allen reminisces about some of the characters he met when he spent the summer of 1937 on the Fegans.

"I remember Old Ominous best. He was a hunch-backed Texan, a really mean guy. He'd be talking away to you, saying something nasty about someone, and he'd stick his knife down his shirt and scrape the dirt off his back. We swapped him one of our rowboats for his canoe, a narrow little thing you could hardly put your bum into. I fitted it with an outrigger and Betty fished out of that. He put a little cabin on the rowboat and took off out into the strait. It was blowing like stink, and he was never seen again."

"Maybe he'll turn up one day," suggests Sharie.

"Maybe. He'd be about a hundred and twenty by now, though. Did I tell you about the crippled German? I met him here, too. He'd been to the library and read accounts by Spanish explorers about a ten-mile-long island with treasure hidden in caves at its northern end. He was convinced it had to be Lasqueti. Then this guy who was on his way north in a canoe to pan for gold turned up. He had a miner's lamp, so the German asked him and I to go and look for the caves. We took Barrie with us, he was only three years old then. We bushwhacked, and we found the cave entrance. We left Barrie outside and told him not to move and we crawled down. The passage opened up into a cavern, and more passages led off that. I wanted to carry on, but the other guy was sweating and shaking, he said we should go back in case Barrie hurt himself. I wasn't a bit scared, but that was because I was too young and inexperienced."

The Fegan Islands are uninhabited now; none of the old characters are left, and nothing remains of their shacks. Over on the shores of Lasqueti, half a mile away, there's not a light to be seen.

"No one out here except us chickens," says Sharie ruefully.

"And mosquitoes," I add.

Clouds of mosquitoes are descending on us, making us curse our decision not to bring a net. Sharie has one that she rigs up over her bunk, to cover her face and shoulders. Allen, in the fore cabin, doesn't bother protecting himself.

"They prefer Sharie," he says. "They fly right by my porthole and to her end of the boat."

JUNE 24 ■ Just before dawn, we're wakened by the movement of the boat. A swell is rolling into our anchorage, and soon Allen calls, "Should we go, Dag? Maybe we better get out of here before it gets any worse."

We begin the now familiar scramble to hoist the sail and stow away our gear. The overcast sky is the colour of pewter, and a stiff north wind is whipping up steep, four- to five-foot waves. Heeling over hard, *Luna Moth* bucks her way through them around the northern tip of Lasqueti.

"This is great, like riding a wild horse!" Dag cries.

I sit next to him in tense silence, gazing at the turbulent sea as we scoot around Spring Bay Point. It's six o'clock before we skirt Marine Island and drop anchor close to *China Cloud,* in the quiet waters of Maple Bay. After a breakfast of eggs and bacon, and two pots of tea, we go back to bed.

"Hello sleepyheads!" calls Allen a few hours later, when he and Sharie row alongside in the dory. "Want to go and get your new mast?"

There are no "Private" signs on Marine Island, and its only development is a large tent platform in a meadow of rose campion. A steep path leads up from the pebble beach into a forest. At the head of the beach Sharie sits on a log.

"I'm feeling dizzy," she says. "I'll wait for you all here."

"Honey, your heartbeat was up this morning," Allen protests. "You need some exercise, you've got to keep going!"

Since Sharie had a pacemaker installed in 1988, Allen has been keeping a careful check on her heart. He recently bought a digital machine to monitor her pulse and blood pressure, and he makes sure she gets regular exercise. Grasping her by the hand, he pulls her up the path, while I follow close behind, ready to catch her if she falls.

As we wind our way through the forest, Allen keeps pausing to break twigs and mark our route. He's looking about intently, searching for something.

"See that?" he says, pointing to a stump. "The rest of the tree is the foremast on *China Cloud.* Your mast is close by—I remember noticing it when I was here last year, and thinking it would be just the right size."

Within minutes he's found the tree, a straight red cedar, and is sizing it up. Its diameter near the ground is about five inches. Then he paces back, trying to guess at its height.

"I can't tell from here," he says finally. "I'll have to go up it."

Gripping the trunk with his hands and his bare feet, he begins to climb it, the way boys in the tropics climb coconut palms. Lithe and loose as a monkey, he goes higher and higher, stepping on thin branches that crack ominously beneath his weight. I watch in awe, and a certain amount of shame, as this incongruously fit eighty-three-year-old scales the skinny tree. It's a feat I wouldn't have attempted when I was in my twenties, never mind now. And I certainly won't be trying it in forty years' time, when I'm the same age as Allen.

Once he's near the top, Allen fishes round in his pocket for a measuring tape and drops one end for Dag to read.

"Thirty-feet five, Allen. Perfect."

He shinnies down, and leaps the last few feet to the ground. "Well, what are we waiting for?" he asks, dusting off his hands.

Using Allen's saw, Dag cuts through the trunk. It gives way with creaking and splintering sounds, a rushing of branches through foliage and finally a THUMP! as it hits the ground. Grabbing his axe, Allen starts furiously chopping off limbs, then peeling away the bark in long strips, revealing the slick, pale yellow wood beneath. Finally the two men roll the tree to the edge of the bluff and push it over. It slides down to the beach, where Dag will return over the next few days to smooth and shape the tree into our new mast.

JUNE 25 ■ At high tide we sail between Lasqueti and Lindburg islands, along a channel so narrow that overhanging trees scrape *China Cloud*'s masts, and into Scottie Bay. According to Allen, this bay is one of the most protected anchorages around Lasqueti Island. At its northern end, where we anchor, the air is completely still, and heat seems to radiate from Lindburg's sandstone bluffs.

"Want to go for a row?" asks Allen. "I'll show you where *China Cloud* was born."

He helps Sharie climb down into the dory, I follow her, and then he leaps in next to us, perfectly balanced. Towards the southern end of the

Squitty Bay, from where Allen fished in the 1930s.

bay is the Lasqueti Island Fish Company. Herring skiffs are pulled up on the beach, and a couple of large seiners are tied up at the dock. It was because of Tom Millicheap, one of the founders of this company, that *China Cloud* was built nearby. In 1980, Allen was recovering from a nervous breakdown which he'd suffered the year before when he and Sharie were sailing in Mexico. To stop himself from brooding, he threw himself into making plans for another boat.

"I was reading about junks. They looked so pretty and I thought that a boat that could go high and dry would be good for this coast. So I started building a model. Sharie saw it and said, 'Oh no, not again!' We were anchored here in *Native Girl* and Tom Millicheap came over one day and said, 'So what are you doing, having a rest after your trip?' I told him I was looking for a place to build a boat and he pointed over to this grassy place by one of his sheds and said, 'Help yourself!' By the end of that day I had the place all cleared and I was making steps up to it, and next day we had poles cut and were building the shed."

He rows into a small cove, bounded by smooth rocks, on the Lasqueti Island side of the bay.

"That's where we built *China Cloud*," he says, pointing up into the trees.

There's little trace of the site. The boat shed is gone, the skids down the steep slope are overgrown, the steps have crumbled away. Every day, for two and a half years, Allen worked here and Sharie rowed to and from *Native Girl* with food, and to collect him for his afternoon nap. Two and a half years of hard, relentless labour—done by a man who was then seventy years old.

"Being with you makes me feel that my life still stretches a long, long way ahead," I tell him.

"I wish someone could make me feel like that," he answers sadly.

J U N E   2 6   ■   "When this book is published," says Allen, "make sure they include the lines of *China Cloud*. Then I won't always have to be making photocopies to send to people who write and ask for them."

Allen is as generous with his ideas as with everything else. When a friend recently told him that some designers destroy the lines, or plans, of their boats, so that they can't be copied, he was deeply shocked. He's not sure exactly how many replicas of *China Cloud* are being built right now. Two are under construction on Lasqueti Island, and one of these is close by, here in Scottie Bay.

We row to shore, clamber up the rocks, and walk along a path flanked by long grasses and blackberry bushes. From behind a fence of weathered beachcombed wood comes a deep, drawling voice: "Whose this ah hear coming up mah path?"

A big man dressed in long loose shorts and a baggy t-shirt appears, and enfolds Allen and Sharie in a bear hug. Bill Wilkinson has a seafaring past: he grew up in Chesapeake Bay, Virginia, where he worked on lobster boats before beginning a career piloting vessels into Maryland waters. He met the Farrells in 1980 when he was visiting Lasqueti Island and they were building *China Cloud*. Several visits and eight years later, he had given up his job, moved to Lasqueti and was making plans to build his own *China Cloud*.

The boat sits in a long draughty shed with a tarp roof, looking for all the world like an ark in progress. Allen leaps around her, as excited as a five-year-old, his face animated and his eyes alight. But Bill is more subdued. He came here to fulfil a dream, but instead got a hefty dose of reality. He long ago realized that, despite all his power tools, he could never build a boat as fast as Allen. He doesn't have his experience, or his innate judgement.

"Allen knows if things are right just by looking," he tells me. "One time, he stood staring at the sheer, that curve along the top of the hull. He said something was wrong, but he wasn't sure exactly what. When we measured up, one side was out by about a quarter of an inch."

The physical aspect of the task is also taking its toll. Bill gets arthritis in his hands, and working in this cold shed all winter long is impossible for him. And increasingly he's feeling the weight of loneliness, living alone and facing this huge project without a partner.

"It must be so hard on your own," Sharie empathizes. "Allen did nothing else but work when he was building *China Cloud,* but he had me to look after him."

"You need a Sharie," I tell Bill.

He smiles sadly.

"I sure do."

JUNE 27 ■ All day long, Allen and Sharie have visitors who arrive in rowboats, motorboats, canoes, a kayak. We leave them in peace, and spend some quiet time on our own. Dag collects seaweed, and spreads it out over the rocks on shore to dry. I do laundry, washing and rinsing the clothes in saltwater, and hanging them from the rigging. Then I swim over to Lindburg Island clutching a bottle of shampoo between my teeth. After lathering my hair, I float about on my back ducking my head under the water until all the soap is gone. Hauling myself onto a boulder, I stretch out, cover my face with my arm and doze off. A loud splash wakes me. I open my eyes to see a kingfisher fluttering up from the surface of the water. It flies to an arbutus tree leaning over the bay, alights on a branch and whacks the small fish in its beak against the red bark. From the forest comes the sound of excited, high-pitched cheeping, and in a flash the kingfisher has disappeared, off to feed its hungry family.

We've just begun feasting on clams that Dag dug up over by Marine Island, when an osprey starts fishing around *Luna Moth.* Time and time again it hovers above the deep, dark green water, as if admiring its reflection, before swooping with a vengeance, and grabbing a glittering fish with its talons. We watch, our supper forgotten, hardly daring to breathe.

JUNE 28 ■ Visitors continue to arrive on *China Cloud,* bringing with them food from their gardens, some of Lasqueti's recent gossip and stories from its past. One story concerns Henry Wagner, who in 1912 moved with his wife and three young children into a shack in Scottie Bay, close to Bill Wilkinson's place. Lasqueti Island has long had the reputation of being a place to lay low, away from the eyes of the law, and this is exactly what Wagner was doing. He was an infamous criminal wanted throughout the States, where he was known as the "Flying Dutchman." He and his accomplice Bill Julian, who lived nearby, were regularly crossing the strait by night in a twin-engined boat called the *Spray,* robbing stores and post offices in small coastal communities, then returning to hide their booty in the woods. One night in March 1913, Wagner's wife begged him not to leave with Julian, as she had had a premonition that something would befall him and he would not return. He chose to ignore her, and set off with Julian for Union Bay where, while robbing the Fraser and Bishop Store, they were surprised by two policemen. Wagner shot and killed one policeman before being overpowered by the other. Julian managed to escape, and rowed the *Spray's* dinghy back to Lasqueti across a storm-swept Georgia Strait, only to be arrested the next day. For their crimes, Julian went to jail for five years, and Wagner was hanged in Nanaimo. Their booty, rumoured to still be buried somewhere around Scottie Bay, has yet to be found.

Another visitor talks of Sideris, a self-styled guru who moved here in the sixties, built a stone house in Long Bay and established a commune. Rumours spread that members of his commune were rustling island cattle and sheep. Then one of the group fell out with Sideris and went to the police on Vancouver Island, offering to show them where the bones of rustled cattle were buried. The court case that ensued was dismissed due to inconclusive evidence, and the defence lawyer got paid in part with Lasqueti Island screech. Sideris left for Calvert Island, and,

Fishing boats in Scottie Bay, Lasqueti Island.

according to some versions of this story, his followers were "escorted" to the ferry by a posse of local men, who made sure they got on it. The stone house was abandoned. A few people tried to live there before it was eventually destroyed by fire, but had never stayed long.

"We went there once," says Allen. "The inside walls were covered in fir shakes and there was a stone fireplace so big you could walk into it. But the vibes were horrible; it was a spooky house. We know one couple who spent a night there and got so scared they slept in the hen house."

Some of the latest island gossip concerns someone who has left his wife of many years for a woman half his age.

"He can't help it, it's all because of gonads," insists Allen. "But why cause so many problems? Why can't they just spend a couple of nights together, and get everything out of their systems?"

"Maybe you should go over to see them, and impart this wisdom," I tease him.

"Not me!" he chuckles. "I'm not getting involved!"

JUNE 29 ■ Dag tows the newly finished mast over from Marine Island, and hoists it into place with Allen's halyard. The job is done quickly and easily, though Dag fears the mast is too loose in the step, and hammers in wedges of wood to secure it. He leaves our old mast for Bill Wilkinson to use—with luck, it might one day be part of his *China Cloud*.

A northwest wind is blowing out in the strait; it's a glorious day for sailing, and we set off south, towards Rouse Bay. We're past Jervis Island and almost in Bull Passage by the time the wind drops, but we continue to slowly move, drifting with the current at a little more than a knot. Jedediah Island, newly designated a park, slips by, and then Bull Island. We bask in the sunshine, enjoying the wild landscapes on either side of the channel: rocky bluffs sprouting wind-bent juniper trees and bright flowers, little beaches tucked away in half-hidden coves, fantastically sculpted boulders.

As we approach Rouse Bay I read aloud to Dag from Elda Copley Mason's book about Lasqueti Island, and the account of her family's arrival here in 1916. The bay seems to have changed little since then—it is still wrapped around with dense forest, and overlooked by only one small house. When we go ashore we quickly find the creek Mason describes, the small meadow up from the beach, the remains of her family's old vegetable gardens and the patches of wild blackberries, which are just starting to ripen. An overgrown, grassy path behind the house leads through stands of old trees and moss-covered nurse logs. Tall foxgloves bloom all over the forest floor, some of them brilliantly illuminated by sunlight shafting through the canopy.

"In 1972 we spent a week rowing around Lasqueti," says Sharie, "and we stopped off here for a night. The people in the house invited us to stay. In the morning we collected salal berries and made pancakes for everyone, then got a boatload of seaweed for the garden."

Allen's memories of Rouse Bay go back to 1940, when Japanese fish buyers were anchored here in a scow, and seiners like the one Allen worked on for a while came in to sell their catch. But long before all of this, a couple called Margaret and William Rouse lived here, and created gossip as juicy as any going about today on Lasqueti Island. Sometime around 1895, William Rouse swapped wives with a

neighbour, Harry Higgins. By all accounts, this arrangement was ami-
cably made, and was agreeable to all concerned. Margaret Rouse, who
was fifty-three years old, went to live with Harry in his house facing the
Finnerty Islands. Nineteen-year-old Mary Ann Higgins, who grew up
in Maple Bay and had been married off to Harry five years before,
became the new Mrs. Rouse. She left her son Charlie for Harry and
Margaret, and took her daughter to Rouse Bay, where she proceeded to
give birth to three more girls in quick succession.

"Why can't people sort themselves out like that these days?" asks
Allen, when I recount the story.

We share a supper of red snapper, which Dag just caught from the
kayak. Then Allen records the temperature of the water and air—sixty-
eight and eighty-two degrees—and announces that finally it's warm
enough for him to go swimming. Stripping off all his clothes, he dives
in from the deck of *China Cloud*. Meanwhile, Sharie dons her new,
brightly coloured swimsuit.

"I feel conspicuous in it," she admits to me, as she climbs carefully
down the wooden ladder.

"She was trying on a plain dark blue suit," calls Allen from where
he's floating on his back, "and it made her look so pale. I persuaded her
to buy this one instead. It cost eighty dollars! And then she got new sandals that cost *a hundred and fifty dollars!* We've never spent that much on
clothes in our entire lives. We usually buy everything in thrift stores."

"But the sandals are so comfortable," Sharie reminds him, "and the
girl in the shop told me they're such good quality, they should last me
the rest of my life." She pauses, thinking about what she's just said, then
throws back her head and laughs heartily.

China Cloud *returns to Nanaimo Harbour, after a winter's absence.*

China Cloud *running wing and wing.*

Summer at last! Allen and Sharie enjoy the sunshine on China Cloud.

China Cloud *at anchor in Echo Bay, Newcastle Island.*

Luna Moth *moored off Protection Island, waiting for the voyage to begin.*

Dag makes repairs on the mast.

Halcyon days on China Cloud.

Curious Mario pokes his head through the porthole.

China Cloud*'s tender on the beach in Clam Bay.*

Ted Long bades us farewell on Ruxton Island.

Dawn breaks over Valdes Island.

Ocean Girl.

The boat sheds in Hope Bay, North Pender Island.

Allen takes Sharie and Lois for an evening row.

Shack Islands, Piper's Lagoon: The remains of fishermens' shacks from the 1930s.

Allen prepares to change anchorage in Bargain Harbour.

CHAPTER FIVE

South Texada Island to Smuggler Cove

JUNE 30 ■ At dawn Dag goes off in the kayak to explore the little islet at the mouth of Rouse Bay. He's soon back, with a pained expression on his face. We were halfway down Bull Passage yesterday when he remembered he'd left his only pair of shoes on Marine Island. Now he's going barefoot, hoping that the soles of his feet will soon be as tough as Allen's. Evidently they're not tough enough for the prickly pear cacti that creep along the ground, all over the islet.

"Quick, give me the tweezers," he begs, as he climbs aboard *Luna Moth*.

By eight o'clock, the temperature is already in the mid-seventies. Allen rows out to check the wind in Sabine Channel and returns with reports of a northwesterly.

"But it often changes when you get around the tip of Texada Island. It can be blowing like stink down Sabine and flat calm out in the strait. Shall we try and get over to the mainland? We'll head down to Smuggler Cove and wait there for a southeaster."

We have a smooth sail over to the south end of Texada Island. Its shoreline is steep and rugged, exposed to the southeast winds that arrive with a vengeance after their long fetch up the strait. I tell Dag about Elda Copley Mason's account of her family rowing here from Lasqueti Island in 1916 to visit a friend's homestead in a place she called Whitaker Bay.

"A homestead along here?" Dag peers up at the dark rock buttresses. "I can't imagine it."

Minutes later we sail by a tiny cove, no more than a slot in the cliff. Above a narrow beach are a few weathered buildings and old fences, and a steep field leading up to woods. There's no sign of anyone, no movement. It looks like a ghostly, long-abandoned place. A puff of wind reaches *Luna Moth*'s sails, the cliffs close round the cove once more, and the settlement is gone, leaving us wondering if perhaps we imagined it.

To the south, beyond the white bluffs of Thormanby Island, the Coast Range mountains are muted and softened by the heat haze, and fade away against the bleached sky. As we approach the buoy off Upwood Point, the view along the coast to the north unrolls. Here the scene is all drama, layer upon layer of jagged mountains, some rising blue black from the ocean, those more distant so pale and translucent it seems I can see one mountain through another. In the mouth of majestic Jervis Inlet sits Nelson Island, dark and brooding. Soon we'll be sailing along these shores, as far as Desolation Sound. Seeing our route spread out before us, I'm suddenly impatient, wanting the wind to blow harder so that we can get on with the journey ahead.

As if to teach me a lesson, the wind dies. By ten o'clock we are drifting south with the current. Dag throws out a fishing line. Allen and Sharie sit at the tiller of *China Cloud,* practising their Spanish. Presently, when a cat's paw ripples the water, Allen turns the boat and sails back towards the tiny cove where we saw the old homestead.

"What's going on?" says Dag in amazement. "It's not like Allen to anchor in such an exposed place."

By the time we raft up alongside *China Cloud,* the Farrells are having their lunch.

"Our friend Jimmy Dougan lived in this homestead," Allen explains, when we join them below decks. "I thought you might like to see the place. I knew Jimmy's dad in the forties. He was logging here on Texada, around the corner in Anderson Bay, and he used to come over sometimes to Pender Harbour. When I first saw Jimmy he was a tiny baby. He grew up, came here, got married, and had four kids. His wife left him—I guess it got too lonely for her. Poor Jimmy, I wonder where he is now."

He leans over to a cupboard at the end of the bench, searches around among papers and books and pulls out a cassette tape.

"He's a wonderful singer and guitarist. He writes all his own songs, and he performs at dances all around here. He sent us this tape once. Do you want to hear it?" Seconds later, the cabin is filled with Jimmy Dougan's rich, rolling voice.

A little up north where the eagle soars, far away from the city smog,
I built a shack in a rocky cove from the driftwood board and log.
My soul was tired and my heart was down
From trudging through the dreary grind,
So I left it all and I asked old God to teach me peace of mind.

On the winter nights when the southeast howls
And the waves come crashing in,
I think about the friends I've had and the places that I've been.
I dream about the women I've loved and the one that I can't get back,
Then I write my songs and I thank old God
That I'm safe in my cosy shack.

And the southeast howls and soothes me,
 and the southeast swells roll high,
And the Georgia Strait is a mighty sure
 fate, if you're looking for a way to die,
If you're looking for a way to die.

By the time the song is over, Allen is looking decidedly nervous.

"I don't want to be stuck here if the wind switches. And there's a southeasterly feel to the air. Oh brother! We'll have our nap and then we'll go."

While they sleep, Dag and I take the dory ashore. The narrow beach is littered with evidence of the ferocity of winter storms. Huge silvered logs have been tossed high, and lie in jumbled heaps. Among them are alarming bits of flotsam—a couple of old doors with twisted, bent hinges, some roofing shingles, a mangled outboard engine. Sitting high and dry among barnacle-covered rocks is a stout boat, anchored to the

Anchored in Whitaker Bay.

cliffs by three hefty lines. A boardwalk leads past a couple of sheds and a house with shake-covered walls. Several pairs of children's shoes are on the doorstep of the house, and through a window I glimpse dishes in a drying rack, a book lying open on a table. Though the homestead obviously isn't abandoned, an eerie silence hangs over it. We go through a creaking gate and up a steep meadow towards stands of big, well-spaced firs and alders. A ravine runs through them, its bed dry. I can imagine this place in winter, the relentless rushing of a swollen creek, the waves crashing on the beach, the wind whistling in from the ocean and up through these trees. But now, all is quiet, save for the cawing of a few crows, the cry of seagulls, the crackle of dried rock moss under our feet.

"I feel like we're intruding on something," says Dag. "Let's go back to the boat."

We quietly tie up the dory and creep across the deck of *China Cloud* so as not to disturb Allen and Sharie, then lie down for a nap ourselves. I've barely shut my eyes before there's a whistling call from shore. Looking out, I see a lanky man and two children standing by the water's edge, as if they've materialized from nowhere.

"Must be ghosts," murmurs Dag sleepily. "You go and see who they are."

In silence, the three figures stand and watch me paddle towards them.

"Are you Jimmy?" I hesitantly call out to the man.

"That's me, ma'am."

He's dark-eyed and bearded. Suspenders loop over his bare shoulders and hold up his pants. The boys next to him are about eight or nine years old, and could be twins. They run forward, pointing to the best place for me to steer the kayak among the barnacle-covered rocks. As I climb out, the man steps forward and takes my hand.

"You smell like almonds," he says, sniffing the air around me. "The way people smell is very important. It's the same way with houses, some of them you walk into and feel comfortable right away, and it's the smell, even though you might not recognize what it is. Now, take off those sunglasses so I can see your eyes. That's the best way to get to know a person."

Very soon, I know a great deal about Jimmy Dougan. He grew up on Texada Island, where his father was logging in Anderson Bay. By the mid-sixties he was back at the family home in Cobble Hill, on Vancouver Island, working as a mechanic. But he missed Texada, and had a yen to live more simply. In 1966 he arrived here and, like the Whitakers sixty years before, started beachcombing for his building materials, and scratching a garden out of the meagre soil.

"I told everyone I was going to homestead and survive off twelve dollars a month. They all said I was crazy. They were right, I guess, but I was twenty-one years old and idealistic. I did everything the hard way. The wood that gets washed up on the beach is often full of nails and spikes, so I pulled those out and straightened them. I cut planks with a power saw and I split shakes. Sometimes people gave me stuff. What's part of my house now used to be a horse barn. It came from Cook Bay—Frank Corbett gave it to me and I towed it here over the drink. Everything's log and shacky, and I don't have the wherewithal to make things pretty, but that's the way I chose."

Jimmy soon grew lonely in Whitaker Bay, and placed a lonely hearts advertisement in a farming newspaper.

"I said I was looking for a girl between eighteen and twenty-five. She had to be a Christian, a non-smoker, and beautiful."

Margaret, an eighteen-year-old farm girl from Alberta, began corresponding with him. After six months she came out for a visit, and two days later they were engaged.

"So what you see here was a team effort," he says, as we walk up to the house, where he's invited me in for tea. "There was the two of us, and then the four kids. We kept goats, had a garden. But since my wife left it's been hard keeping this place together by myself. The eldest girl is married now, and has a baby of her own. I home-school the other three and we mostly stay in the Coxes' place, a couple of bays over, where I keep a horse for them. Sometimes we stay in Pender Harbour; I rent my friend Luella's place there."

Elder, the youngest of the two boys, runs to a shed behind the house and returns with a bamboo cage, which he holds aloft for me to see. It's rectangular in shape, with a hinged top and wire looped around two of the bars to form handles. Lining the bottom is some plastic-covered foam. Elder and his brother Charles jump about excitedly, asking me to guess what it's for.

"Birds?" I venture.

"It's a crib!" announces Jimmy proudly. "I designed and built it myself. You put the little 'un inside and you can hand it from one boat to another, no matter how much the waves are tossing you about."

Inside the house, his daughter Trina is sitting on the sofa reading a book. She's in her early teens, and she constantly rolls her eyes as Jimmy continues with his stories.

"So you heard one of my tapes? I've got a couple of records out on my own label, Skinny Jimmy's Snack Bar. I've been on TV and radio, but I haven't hit the big time yet. Right now I'm working as a monkey wrencher, repairing engines for Cox's Logging, over in Anderson Bay.

One of these days I'll find a new woman, someone smart, with business sense. She'll do the managing side and I'll write more songs and put out more records and we'll sell them on the TV."

Through the window, we can see Allen, Sharie and Dag climbing down into the dory and setting off towards the beach.

"Allen's a real artist," says Jimmy. "He's got imagination, and without that you can't think properly. We always argue about politics, though, because I'm a real Van der Zalm man, and he's a socialist. But we like each other—the right and the left have more in common than Allen realizes."

When Allen arrives, he's too concerned about the wind to talk politics, or to accept Jimmy's invitation to stay for dinner. Jimmy tunes into a weather station, and we listen to a report forecasting several more days of northwesterlies.

"I don't know about that," says Allen, worriedly glancing out of the window. "It feels a bit southeasterly to me."

As we walk back towards the beach, Allen asks Jimmy if he's lonely here on the south end of Texada.

"I couldn't have stayed in the humdrum," he answers. "I'm living the way I always wanted to, and I've got no regrets. But I don't want to die. A person's only ready to die when heartache, frustration and fed-up-ness come to a pinnacle in their life. And I'm not there yet."

"Neither am I, Jimmy," says Allen. "But I'm going to die soon anyway."

"In your case, Allen," counters Jimmy, "it's not a case of when you die but *if* you die!"

By five o'clock a few puffs of wind have pushed us around Upwood Point. Half an hour later, we're totally becalmed once more, and the Strait of Georgia looks like a huge, glassy lake. Allen drops the thermometer overboard.

"The water's seventy-five degrees!" he calls over, then strips off and dives in.

Soon we're all swimming, and moving faster than our abandoned boats. When we haul ourselves aboard once more, both Dag and Allen start yulohing towards Anderson Bay. A large power launch flying an American flag comes around the point, and heads straight for us. On deck are several people with video cameras glued to their faces. When the launch is almost alongside *China Cloud,* they slowly lower their cameras, revealing stunned expressions, as they realize that the old man rowing the Chinese junk is completely naked save for a sun visor. The launch's engines growl as it makes a fast turn and zips away, leaving us rocking uncomfortably in its wake.

"Oh brother," says Allen, as we tie up either side of an enormous boom stick in Anderson Bay. "If the wind switches to southeast tonight, we're in trouble."

The bay is long and narrow, and faces south along the strait. At its head is a cleared area with a house and a dirt road leading up into the forest. Elsewhere, the shore is steep and rocky.

"See where the trees start, way up there?" says Allen, pointing to the top of the bluff close to where we're anchored. "That's where the waves get to."

He knows the bay well. In the forties he often fished around here from his gas boat, and recalls one day when he caught three hundred pounds of cod in one hour.

"I got ten cents a pound for them—that was wealth!"

He also remembers the logging camp which Jimmy's grandfather established in 1942, and which ran for twenty-three years. Old Mr. Dougan had been approached by Nanaimo logging baron Ole Buck, who had purchased two blocks of virgin timber on the south end of Texada and wanted someone to clear them for him. In his autobiography, *My Daughter's Request,* Jimmy's father, Charles, describes Anderson Bay when he first arrived here on barges loaded with logging equipment. It was, he writes, "a rugged virgin piece of wilderness . . . that had never been violated by any men or machines." On the beach he found huge pieces of driftwood, and the skeleton of a large whale.

This paradise was soon transformed. The first trees were felled and the land around the bay cleared and flattened for a camp. Bunkhouses were set up, pits were dug for latrines, a water line was strung from the creek, and, as this was before the days of the power saw, a cabin for the saw filer was built. A well-known local character called Jack Wray was employed to do the booming, a pile driver and crew were brought in, "and the cockles and clams had the peace and tranquillity of their sandy home disturbed for the first time."

Allen Farrell collection

Crossing Malaspina Strait on Ocean Girl, *with a friend of the Farrells at the helm.*

Until the late fifties, there was no road from Anderson Bay to the north end of Texada Island, and its nearest point of contact with the outside world was Pender Harbour, a port of call for Union Steamships. Dougan describes how loggers hitched rides there on gas boats—first on Jack Wray's *Susie Q,* then in the company's own twelve- by thirty-six foot scow, *Texada Queen.*

"Well, well, fancy old Dougan writing a book," chuckles Allen, paging through the copy of *My Daughter's Request* that Jimmy had given me that afternoon. "Look, here's Jimmy and his family!"

I lean over to see the small black and white photograph, taken outside the house in Whitaker Bay. With suspenders holding up his trousers and a narrow beard creeping round his chin, Jimmy looks much the same as he does now. Two small children sit at his feet. The pretty woman next to him looks strangely familiar, and I wrack my brains to think why, until I realize that the face gazing from the page is a carbon copy of Jimmy's shy teenage daughter, Trina.

Heading towards Smuggler Cove.

J U L Y   1   ■   While we eat breakfast, Mario gazes down at us from the deck of *China Cloud,* mewing plaintively.

"I think he's feeling strange, being back on Texada," muses Sharie.

When Keray was living on the island in 1981, he found Mario running around wild. Allen and Sharie were adamant they didn't want a cat, until the day Keray turned up with the fluffy little kitten.

"Bloody thing!" cries Allen from the aft deck. "He's shit in the cockpit again. He's mewing because he knows he's in trouble."

"Poor pussy," coos Sharie, gathering Mario into her arms. "He senses that we're planning to leave him soon."

At eight, we untie our boats from the boom stick, raise the sails, and drift out. *China Cloud* slips by, so close I can hear Allen humming at the tiller and the rattle of dishes as Sharie washes up after breakfast. At the mouth of the bay we manoeuvre through a narrow, rocky channel between the shore and a small island. Out in the strait the wind is blowing from the northwest at a good fifteen knots, and the sea is flecked with white. I pull the kayak aboard and dress in waterproof clothing, anticipating a cool, wet crossing to Smuggler Cove. When we're less than half a mile from Texada, however, the wind drops, the whitecaps

die down, and the tide begins to pull us south. Then we get a southerly breeze. It blows and dies alternately, teasing us until half past eleven,
when it switches back to a steady northwest. Now that he's got a new
mast, and is able to use his full sail area, Dag is unwilling to reef down.
We bowl towards the mainland, almost keeping pace with *China Cloud*.

"Yesterday I overheard you telling Allen you didn't know how much
wind it would take to capsize the boat!" I yell at him, as waves slop over
the deck. But he's far too exhilarated to pay me any heed.

The narrow entrance of Smuggler Cove leads into a delightful maze
of islets, protected little bays and rocky beaches. The cove got its name
from two reputed smuggling operations. Chinese labourers left unemployed after the completion of the Canadian Pacific Railway at the end
of last century, and banned from entering the States, were said to have
been run across the border from here by Larry Kelly. And during
American prohibition in the twenties, liquor illegally manufactured on
Texada Island was apparently stored here before being smuggled into
the States on fast boats.

In 1971 the bay and the land around it were designated a provincial
park, but people owning the handful of cottages on the islets were
allowed to retain lifetime occupancy.

"When Betty and I got here in 1934, an old fisherman lived in that
place," says Allen, looking at a tidy little cottage with tubs of flowers on
its deck. "But it wasn't so spruced up back then."

Smuggler Cove was the couple's first stop when they set off up the
coast with their rowboat.

"Jim Warburton suggested we come here. He was a real old salt, a
great big tough guy from Britain with huge hands and wide fingers.
He had an old Japanese fishing boat with a tiny cabin he barely fit
into. You'd come alongside this little boat and big Warburton would
appear from it. He was married to a Haida woman. After his first child
was born, he'd tell people, 'She was lying on the bed and the baby
came out, so I took some sail twine, tied off the cord and cut the little
bugger adrift.' "

As this is the start of a holiday weekend, lots of other boats are
motoring into the cove, and tying lines to shore. The evening is warm
and sunny, and people sit on their decks having predinner drinks. They

smile down at us, ducking under their stern lines as Allen rows us along the shore.

"Funny that you rarely see other boaters just rowing around like this, for a look," I comment.

"I don't understand it," says Allen. "Sharie and I have rowed along the shoreline in the evenings for fifty years now, and we're still not tired of doing it."

Lots of mergansers are about, with families of brand-new chicks. They swim like fury to get away from the dory, going so fast they sometimes moonwalk over the water. Some mothers have chicks nestled on their backs, between their wings. An eagle sits close by on a snag, eyeing the fluffy bundles.

"We once saw an eagle snatch a merganser chick, right here," Allen recalls. "When an osprey buzzed it, the eagle dropped the chick, and it fell in the water and then hopped onto its mother's back and got away safely."

He rows us past an islet covered with juniper trees. Over the years he's often come here to collect "knees," strong, bent sections of trees, for building boats. Sharie recognizes a beach where they once dug clams with two gay friends of hers from Vancouver, Herman and Stuart.

"When I met them I didn't know they were gay," she tells me. "I didn't even know what homosexuality was. Then I fell in love with Stuart and he had to explain it to me."

"When I met Sharie, she fearfully told me about her good friend Stuart, the homosexual," Allen laughs. "She thought I'd be angry but I said, 'So what? It's only natural!' "

Back on *China Cloud* she shows me a photo of Stuart. He was a handsome man, with good bone structure and gentle eyes.

"How did you meet Stuart?" I ask her.

"On *Te Rapunga,* George Dibbern's boat," she answers.

"George was Sharie's true love, before she met me," Allen interjects.

She turns to the shelf behind her and pulls out an old hardback book and a tattered foolscap envelope, stuffed with dog-eared pages.

"George wrote both these books, but only *Quest* got published. I've been meaning to give them to you to read."

Later, on *Luna Moth,* I light the hurricane lamp, curl up in our sleeping bag and open *Quest*. On the title page is an inscription:

The hand-carved snatch block that Allen uses to hoist the anchor.

"Gladys, Who could ever forget gold-shower and lilac in bloom and the song of a Nightingale!?

George Dibbern, Soames Island No 13 Hut, 12th Street, 1918– 1919, 1941–?"

I read and read, until way past midnight.

J U L Y 2 ■ Allen spends most of the day painting and sketching in the main cabin of *China Cloud,* and Dag is off exploring Smuggler Cove by kayak. I read George Dibbern's books, and talk to Sharie over cups of tea, immersing myself in the days before she met Allen, when she was called Gladys Nightingale.

Gladys lived with her parents on Lulu Island and worked as a secretary in Vancouver, first for Granby Consolidated Mining, Smelting and

Power Company, and later for Westinghouse. She danced in her spare time, and befriended musicians, artists and bohemians, people who were seeking to reach beyond the narrow confines of life in the thirties. When the sailor George Dibbern arrived in Vancouver aboard *Te Rapunga,* Gladys was curious about him, and went to visit his boat at the immigration dock, not far from her office.

As a young man, George Dibbern had left his native Germany and sailed all over the world aboard square-riggers. Despite being interned in New Zealand for a year during the First World War, he always dreamed of making that country his home. After the war he returned to Germany, married and had a family. He felt stifled by his life in Germany, by the country's rising tides of fascism and communism, and its mass unemployment. To make ends meet he sold most of his possessions, but refused to part with his thirty-two-foot ketch, *Te Rapunga.* Although the literal translation of this Maori name is "Dark Sun," the meaning can be interpreted as the first indication of dawn after a dark night, or as longing. Both were apt for Dibbern, who wrote in *Quest,* "Perhaps, with the launching of my boat my life really started."

Leaving his family behind, he set sail for the Mediterranean, and from there journeyed across the Atlantic, through the Panama Canal, and down to the South Pacific. Finally he reached New Zealand, only to discover that during his absence the place had changed, and people he loved had died. Declaring himself a citizen of the world, he set sail again, and headed north.

When Gladys stepped aboard *Te Rapunga,* Dibbern was instantly attracted to her. "She moved so gracefully," he wrote, "she had such a sincere and warm-hearted way about her." And she had found herself a free spirit, a man of vision. Right from the start of their relationship, however, Dibbern made it clear that they could never marry, as he hoped one day to be reunited with his wife and children. Gladys accepted not only this, but also his close friendship with Eileen Morris, the young girl who had crewed on *Te Rapunga* from New Zealand.

"George could never really commit himself to anyone," she tells me over afternoon tea. "He was always very clear about that."

Gladys and Eileen became friends, and together helped George complete the manuscript of *Quest.* They went sailing with him up the coast and between them bought land in Galley Bay where, with George, they made plans to establish an artists' community. Their dream was crushed when the Second World War broke out, and Dibbern was expelled from Canada. Gladys sailed with him and Eileen to San Francisco, and there they parted company.

"She could have come voyaging with us if she had wished," he wrote, "but she did not feel that sailing was her life."

"It was more than that," says Sharie. "I loved George, but by then I'd realized that he wasn't the right man for me."

They never met again. When Dibbern reached New Zealand he was again interned on Soames Island, this time for five years. During his imprisonment, *Quest* was published, and he wrote *Ship Without A Port*. After his release, he and Eileen had a child. Then he won a lottery and bought an island off Tasmania, hoping to set up an artists' community there. When this didn't work out he set sail for Germany, but was hit by hurricanes which capsized *Te Rapunga* a total of three times. After surviving many dramas at sea, George returned to New Zealand and died on land, of a heart attack.

By then, Gladys Nightingale had become Sharie Farrell and sailing, after all, was her life.

CHAPTER SIX

Pender Harbour

JULY 3 ■ Taking advantage of a southeast breeze, we sail out of Smuggler Cove and north, past Secret Cove and Harness Island, towards Pender Harbour. Gladys Nightingale sailed this way on *Te Rapunga* in 1939, with George Dibbern and Eileen Morris. That same year Allen completed his thirty-five-foot gas boat, *South Wind,* and set off up the coast in her, with plans to fish. After she broke down out in the strait, he managed to make it into Pender Harbour, where the engine died completely. On Beaver Island, also known as Francis Peninsula, Allen and Betty found a log house for sale and decided to buy it. They moved all their belongings into the house, went to Vancouver to sort out their finances and came straight back to complete the deal. By the time they returned, the house had been sold to a British couple, who had already moved in and presumed they had the right to keep Allen and Betty's possessions.

"Like some beautiful curtains we'd made out of yellow cotton, at fifteen cents a yard," Allen says indignantly. "Anyway, those creeps did us a big favour, because instead we bought five acres with three waterfronts on it for $195. I lived there for nine years—the longest I've ever lived anywhere on land."

We're anchored close to his old property, near the head of Bargain Bay, or Bargain Harbour as he and Sharie call it. Canoe Passage, which dries at low tides, connects the bay to the main body of Pender Harbour.

"Old John Wray widened the passage," says Allen. "Before then it was only big enough for an Indian dugout to get through. When we lived here there was no bridge across it. Coming through here at night in my gas boat, it was as dark as the inside of a cow, but I knew where all the rocks were. In the forties we used to dig clams along here but now . . ."

There's no need for him to finish his sentence. Signs posted on the shore warn against harvesting the shellfish that are now too polluted for human consumption. Big new houses are sprouting up around the bay, and the beaches bristle with private docks.

"It used to be all bush in 1939," says Allen. "Only a few people lived around here. The Wrays and the Warnocks. Luella still lives over there. Her mother, Martha Rouse, was one of the first people here. She married Martin Warnock; he was a beachcomber."

As he talks, pieces of the puzzle fall into place, and I begin making connections between names I have been hearing over the past few weeks. John Wray, whose son was the boomer over in Anderson Bay; Martha, the daughter of the woman who moved across Lasqueti Island and switched from being Mrs. Higgins to Mrs. Rouse; Luella, who rents a house to Jimmy Dougan. When I observe how small the coast is, Sharie laughs heartily.

"It used to be even smaller. You could never go anywhere without getting involved in gossip."

I can imagine intrigues and disputes easily fermenting in Bargain Harbour. From where we're anchored we can't see out to the strait: there's a sense of being enclosed, cut off from the rest of the world. And Pender Harbour's entrance is so obscured by islands that many of the early European explorers sailed right by it, unaware of its protected coves. The first white settlers arrived at the end of last century, attracted by the sheltered waters and the opportunities to fish and log. They established small communities of float houses, and planted gardens and orchards on Francis Peninsula. Herring abounded in the harbour, and before long a herring saltery was towed in. In its wake came Scottish gillnetters and their families who set down in Gerrans Bay, renamed Whiskey Slough because of their hard drinking habits. Tensions soon grew as the local seiners and hand-liners accused the gillnetters of catching too many fish and of depleting the stocks. Sides were taken, and grudges formed that would pass down through generations to come.

As the population of Pender Harbour grew, the Union Steamship started making regular calls at Irvines Landing. But it remained a place that looked in on itself. Until the thirties there was no land access, and only a dirt road for a couple of decades after that. Transportation between its settlements was mostly by boat, earning it the title "Venice of the North."

"When I first came here in 1945 the stores were all on the water, over at Irvines Landing, Pope Landing and Donnelly Landing," Sharie recalls.

Gradually, however, the road was improved and transportation began shifting to the land. Once the steamship service was phased out around 1959, the commercial centre of Pender Harbour switched from Irvines Landing to Madeira Park. The float house settlements disappeared, to be replaced by a plethora of marinas and resorts. Tourism and the real estate business took over from fishing and logging as the mainstays of the economy, and the face of Pender Harbour changed forever.

JULY 4 ■ The sky is low, threatening rain. Dag is in an unsettled mood. He feels too enclosed in Bargain Harbour, and he's bothered by the noise from a house construction site near where we're anchored, and from cars on the bridge spanning Canoe Passage. But the Farrells seem content to stay a while. For them, the bay is full of memories.

"It used to be really beautiful, before they made all these mega-houses," Allen tells us, as we go for our evening row.

The cabin he built in 1939 still peeps from among some trees, up on a bluff. But there's no longer any remnant of the float and fish tanks he constructed on the shore below it. Shortly after he got to Bargain Harbour, he came across the first rowboat he ever built, tied up at Irvines Landing. Five years earlier he'd sold it for ten dollars to a man in Lynnmour, North Vancouver. No one knew how it had ended up here, but he bought it back for fifteen dollars and went out cod fishing.

"I'd put strings through the soft underpart of the cods' jaws, tie them to the boat and tow them home. Sometimes the fish would open their mouths, and put their fins forward against the flow of the water, as if to say, 'I'm not going anyplace!' They made it really hard to row."

Collin Hanney

Kivi *and model of* Ocean Bird, *1953.*

He built himself a sixteen-foot boat with live wells, fished for the Warnocks on their seiners, and did various jobs around Pender Harbour, such as making gun oil from ratfish for a local mechanic, and working at Carter's Boatyard on a point just beyond Canoe Passage. As we row by, he nods towards the small headland covered with scrub trees.

"They called it Padlock Point because Carter used to put padlocks on everything—even his kindling! His ambition was to build a thousand skiffs and rowboats—he made it to nine hundred before he died. So there I'd be at Carter's, sawing away, and I'd see all these free people going through the passage in their fish boats. I couldn't stand working for someone else anymore, so I started building *Kivi,* a twenty-four-foot cod boat with live wells in it. I went rock-cod fishing with a set line, a long line with lots of hooks. I made two or three dollars a day, sometimes only eighty cents. But all the time I was dreaming about the South Seas, so I started work on a boat. I laid a keel with a fir tree and a piece of gumwood, and I thought I'd carry on with it when I got some money or some lumber."

This dream wasn't to come true until after the war, when his marriage to Betty was foundering and he met Sharie. In 1945, she was on a two-week sailing holiday with her friends Joe and Dorothy. Just north of Smuggler Cove, on their way to Joe's place in Pender Harbour, they met Allen in *Kivi*. That evening he visited Sharie at Joe's place and they talked for hours—about boats.

"She told me all about *Te Rapunga* and her trip to San Francisco. She said she had five hundred dollars and asked me to build her a twenty-foot sailboat. I decided she should come and live with me so we could build our own boat, together."

"I ended up seeing a lot of Allen for the rest of that holiday," says Sharie.

"Honey," Allen corrects her, "you saw all of me!"

"Afterwards, I used to come up on the Union Steamship for weekends," she continues. "Allen would pick me up in Halfmoon Bay and we'd stay on *Kivi,* to keep things secret. Betty was still on the scene, in an on and off way. I wouldn't agree to live with him until that was sorted out. It took a few months."

"A few months? It seemed like forever," comments Allen.

"It was really something in those days, for a single woman to go off with a married man. My family were upset, and my friends at work said, 'Fancy Nightie doing that!' And Allen's neighbours here were shocked."

By the time Allen has rowed us back to *China Cloud,* a cool wind is blowing across the bay.

"I'm cold," says Allen, climbing on deck. "I'm always cold. I was shivering the day Sharie met me. She decided to come and keep me warm."

JULY 5 ■ We wake to the call of loons and a sky that looks like grey silk. A family of Canada geese swim around our boat, hoping for crumbs from our breakfast. The chicks, which a few weeks ago were fluffy little bundles, have turned into scruffy, awkward, demanding teenagers. We're leaning over the water to feed them when Dag notices two strange fish nosing around our rudder. While I find our nature guide book, Dag bends over and scoops up one of the fish in his palms. It's shiny green, long and skinny as a snake, with an elongated snout and a spade-shaped tail.

"It's like a Doctor Seuss animal!" cries Dag.

This creature is a pipefish, and a relative of the seahorse. Usually it hides away in eel-grass beds, and is rarely seen. As we marvel over it, its little mouth gasps open and shut. Dag lowers it back into the water, where it makes a beeline for our rudder once more.

Around ten, Allen suggests we all go over to Whiskey Slough, or Gerrans Bay, to see where his Japanese friends the Ikedas and Kawasakis used to live, before the Second World War.

"I remember coming through here in my gas boat in 1941 with Jacky and Cotty Ikeda," he says, as we row along Canoe Passage. "I was bringing them to our house for a visit and the police stopped me and told me I shouldn't be entertaining Japanese. It was awful. People round here said I should have been horse-whipped because I stayed friends with them."

Hostility towards British Columbia's Japanese community—both the Issei who had come from Japan and the Nisei who were born in Canada—had been growing since the end of the century, and was fostered by the activities of the Anti-Asiatic League. The onset of the Depression brought racist feelings to a new high, as the Japanese were blamed for contributing to unemployment and low pay. Hoping to win votes by cashing in on this, the Conservative government introduced laws to disenfranchise Japanese, preventing them from owning land, barring them from government contract work and setting quotas on their fishing licenses. The Japanese responded, as they had throughout the last decades of prejudice, by pulling together.

"And that made people here even madder," says Allen.

They got madder still when, in December 1941, Japan bombed Pearl Harbour and the United States declared war. Within a week, defences were being organized against a possible Japanese invasion along the west coast of Canada. The "Gumboot Navy," a reserve fleet put together from conscripted commercial fishing boats and tugboats, patrolled the coastal waters in search of enemy submarines. When one of these grey-painted boats arrived in Bargain Harbour, Allen feared it had come to conscript local men, and fled into the woods. Later he defended his pacifist beliefs in the face of taunts from local loggers who accused him of not being "red-blooded." And he continued to stand by the Ikedas and Kawasakis as their plight steadily worsened. A curfew was imposed on the Japanese, their organizations and groups were dissolved, their newspapers were banned. All Japanese fishing vessels, thirteen hundred of them, were confiscated and towed to Annieville, near New Westminster, where they were cheaply sold off.

"I remember them coming and towing away the boats," says Allen bitterly. "It was blowing a real strong southeasterly and all the boats were bashing against each other, but they didn't care."

We row past marinas, by large houses with satellite dishes and manicured gardens, then around a point and into Whiskey Slough. The place has a distinctive feel, a sense of the past lingering. There are still a fair number of fish boats anchored here. Thick bush and some dense stands of trees grow along much of the shoreline. Old net sheds and houses stand on barnacle-encrusted pilings, their windows smashed in, fire moss growing from their shingles, and buttercups sprouting from the rotting floats alongside them.

In March 1942, the government announced that for purposes of security all Japanese, including those who had been born in Canada and were full citizens, had to move away from the coast to camps in the interior of B.C.

"It was so awful," says Allen. "Betty and I came here one day, and they were gone. Gone! We felt so sad."

Each family was allowed to take only a small amount of luggage. Stories of their houses being looted and vandalized soon spread, so the Kawasakis got a message to Allen, asking him to move into their house, pack up their belongings and ship them to the interior.

"We lived there for several weeks while we got everything sorted. Months later, a letter came from the family, asking why we hadn't sent them their rice. I thought they were talking about the two pounds of rice we'd found on a shelf in the kitchen, and eaten. It seemed a bit much, considering what we'd done for them, so I didn't reply. Years later I heard that another neighbour had been bragging about the two hundred pounds of rice he'd taken from the Kawasakis' place before I got there. By then I'd lost all contact with them, so I couldn't write and explain. They probably still think it was me who stole their rice."

It was 1949 before the Japanese were allowed to return to the B.C. coast, and another two years before they could fish again. Many of them

Inside Bert Mackay's "museum."

went east, or opted to stay in the interior. Allen's friends never returned to live in Whiskey Slough. The Kawasakis' house is gone now, but the Ikedas' old cabin still stands on pilings over the beach, against a tree-covered cliff.

"I spent a lot of time there with Jacky and Cotty," says Allen, as he rows towards it. "I used to go for dinner, eat seaweed and rice with them, learn Japanese. When they were sent away, Bert Mackay's mother bought the house. I wonder who lives there now."

As we draw closer, a tall, gangly man appears at the side of the house and comes down a set of wooden steps to the water's edge.

"Is that you, Farrell? Come ashore! Come on in!"

Allen squints at the man. "Bert! Well, for heaven's sake. Bert Mackay!"

The two men have known each other since 1939, when Bert was sixteen years old and gillnetting in Bargain Harbour.

"That's the year I caught a thousand fish," he says, chuckling softly. "We sold them by the piece. Five cents for pinks and chinooks, ten cents for chum and thirty-two cents for sockeye. The bigger fish were thrown away, because we didn't get any more for them and they took up too much space. Imagine doing that now!"

His wife, Denise, gives me an amused look.

"These men. They can talk back half a century, remember all the fish they caught, and the way the tide came in on a certain day."

Since Allen was last in the house, in the early forties, a couple of rooms have been added on, and, for Bert's sake, the doorways have been raised. But it's still a tiny place, with low ceilings and windows.

"The kitchen's just the same," says Allen. "Except that it doesn't smell of fish and incense anymore."

His eyes have glazed over, and he wanders in a reverie through to the living room, which is carpeted and filled with heavy furniture, ornaments, books and family photos.

"The walls and the floors were just scrubbed bare wood." His voice is soft, as if he's speaking to himself. "It was clear and uncluttered. Over here, behind the wood stove, there was a wooden bath. They'd fill it with water and you could sit in it up to your neck."

He turns to Bert.

"Do you ever hear from Cotty?"

"Not for a long while. Most of the family live Steveston way now."

As we row back Allen says sadly, "Cotty was lovely. She was my girl-friend for a while. She used to write to me from the interior. Her sister had a goitre because the family couldn't get seaweed out there, and they didn't have enough iodine in their diet. So I collected seaweed, and the Warnocks gave me a big box of salmon for them. I salted the fish and sent it out with the seaweed. The family sent back a big crate of honeydew melons—it was the first time in my life I'd seen them."

JULY 6 ■ Dag and I have returned to Whiskey Slough to see Bert's "museum," which is housed in a shed on one of his four waterfront lots. As he unlocks the door he tells us that for years he's been beachcombing for the glass balls Japanese fishermen used for floats, and has an impressive collection. But this doesn't prepare us for the number of antiques and curios stuffed into this small building. On the first floor, large glass balls in nets hang from the ceiling. Reaching beneath the counters lining the walls, Bert pulls out wheeled boxes, three feet square and full to the brim with hundreds more smaller balls. Spread all over the counters are treasures so numerous it would take days to properly look through them. There's an old crank phone, marine radios from the forties, a 1951 Spilsbury and Tindall radio with channels marked "Government," "Vancouver," "Distress" and "Fish." There are butter boxes and apple boxes from the Union Steamship days, and wooden tubs for churning cream. There are empty bottles which once held Uncle Ben's Malt Liquor and sealed bottles labelled "Good News from God" with "Gospel Tracts Unlimited" inside them. There are old tins of Malkins Ginger and Klim Powdered Milk. There are washtubs and scrubbing boards, a whale eardrum, cookstoves from fishing boats. There's old fishing gear, hunting traps, books, posters; there's even a dusty picture of a young Queen Elizabeth.

"Where on *earth* did you get all this stuff?" I finally exclaim, reeling at the local history spread out before me.

"Oh, here and there," says Bert. "I've been collecting for a long time. Sometimes people come and they're not interested. It's a pleasure to show the likes of you around."

The ground floor is given over to old logging equipment, generators, outboard engines. Bert fires up one of the old Easthopes for us. It splutters into life and starts pounding furiously, spitting out oil and making one hell of a racket.

"You'd hear these all over the harbour in the old days," he yells over the noise. "Don't believe Farrell when he says it used to be nice and quiet around here."

J U L Y   7   ■   This morning I try rowing the dory over to Coho Marina. Allen always makes it look effortless, but I find the oars awkward, and if not handled correctly they easily slip off the pegs that hold them to the boat. He watches me floundering about, trying hard to hide his impatience, and he's visibly relieved when I hand the oars back to him and return to my usual place in the boat, next to Sharie.

Not far from the marina is Madeira Park, a small cluster of shops and businesses, a bank, a school and a post office. We're about to walk into the big IGA supermarket when a brisk young cashier notices the rucksack on my back and the sack over Allen's shoulder, and tells us to leave these by the door. Allen is incensed by this, and loudly pronounces that he won't set foot in the supermarket ever again.

"I'm not eating anything you buy in there," he tells Sharie, who goes in without him. "I'd rather starve!"

"You might change your mind at dinnertime, honey," she says fondly.

On the way back to the dory, Allen trudges along with the sack full of shopping, patently cross with all three of us for our traitorous behaviour.

"Hey, Allen, that cashier didn't notice that I had no shoes on," says Dag, in an effort to cheer him.

When this doesn't work he tries again.

"Allen, did you know that IGA stands for International Gangsters Association?" Allen's face crinkles up; he laughs so hard he has to stop walking, and his disgruntled mood magically evaporates.

As we row away from the marina, Sharie stares up at the clouds.

"I can see trees and roots."

"It's that LSD you took," Allen tells her. "You're having flashbacks."

"LSD?" Dag and I chorus. "When? Where?"

"Oh, right here," he says. "When the hippies were around."

After the Union Steamship stopped running in the late fifties, Pender Harbour's service centre moved to Madeira Park. Irvines Landing quickly went into decline, and the community hall, store, post office and gas station were abandoned. Then came the sixties, and the era of "flower children" seeking a return to the land. Before long the abandoned buildings in Irvines Landing had been rented out to a community of young people.

"We were on *Native Girl*, tied up at Irvines Landing," Allen recalls. "This little boat came in with these great big guys wearing beads and bracelets. One was about eight feet tall. I asked him, 'Are you hippies?' He says, 'Well, you know, some people think that's a bad word.' I helped him tie the boat up, and we started talking about the things you could eat off the land. I took them around the beach and in the woods and showed them mushrooms and goose grass and chicken claws, stuff like that. They ended up living round here. Bill, who owned all the places in Irvines Landing, thought they were real nice people and didn't charge them much rent. But the guys in the beer parlour, the loggers and so on, would come down and throw rocks through their windows. Bill told us, 'I don't know what everyone's going on about, I don't ever see any of that "marry-jew-ana" around.' Poor Bill, that's because he was drunk half the time."

"What about your acid trips?" asks Dag.

"Oh, well, we had a few. One time we went up Pender Hill to take it, and we just seemed to fly down. We tried marijuana, too, but after we'd smoked some we could never remember how to tie knots properly, so we quit."

JULY 8   ■   "I remember Allen walking in his bare feet along this hand rail a few years ago," says Sharie, as we head up the steep ramp of the community dock in Bargain Bay. "An elderly fellow came by in a boat and saw him from behind. Allen's hair was covered by a hat, so the fellow thought he was a teenager or something, and he shouted at him not to be so stupid. When Allen turned around, you should have seen the man's face!"

We're on our way to visit their old friends Collin and Shendra Hanney. Allen and Collin first met in 1939. Collin had recently joined the Kabalarians, a group that believes in the magic power of numbers and words; he changed his name, and persuaded his friends to do likewise. So Mal Daniels became Allen Farrell, Betty became Celeste, and Gladys, when she arrived in Allen's life, became Sharie. By the late fifties Allen and Sharie had become skeptical about numerology, but they've never bothered to revert to their original names.

At the end of a neatly raked dirt path, a door is opened by a small, delicately pretty woman who throws her arms around both the Farrells.

"Come in!" cries Shendra Hanney. "We've just woken up from our nap."

Yesterday, she and Collin returned from this year's shakedown cruise aboard *Balandra,* the wooden boat that Collin built himself and launched in 1945. She lies at anchor below the house, a lovely twenty-three-foot sloop in perfect condition, with the original spruce mast.

"I'd like more time at home in the summer, for the garden's sake," says Shendra. "But Collin wants to be sailing all the time. We're leaving again next week."

In *Once Upon An Island,* author David Conover writes of Collin Hanney sailing up to Wallace Island in 1946 aboard a boat filled with animals. He describes him as a blond-haired, bare-chested "Adonis." At eighty-two, Collin is still handsome, and has a gracious, elegant air.

Wind Song
under construction,
Bargain Harbour,
1947.

Allen Farrell collection

"I owned a pet store in Vancouver called Noah's Ark," he explains, "so that summer I loaded *Balandra* with animals and cruised the Gulf Islands. I had two hundred turtles on board, fish, birds, cats, dogs and some monkeys. The monkeys used to go up the mast—they loved it. It was just a wild idea, but I sold everything, mind you, all except for one dog."

As well as owning a pet shop, over the years Collin has also been a professional violinist, a welder, a photographer and a film-maker. Hanging on the walls of the small living room are some of his photographs, brilliant studies of tribal people he encountered during an expedition to Guatemala, thirty-five years ago. He shows us mementos from that trip: arrows, arrowheads of flint and wood, a club for beating bark to make cloth.

Allen and Sharie linger in the doorway of their old cabin.

"I heard a rumour that you're going to Mexico," he says to Allen, as Shendra hands around herb tea and homemade bread and muffins. He doesn't seem in the least surprised by Allen and Sharie's plan to give up their boat and move south.

"You're used to upheaval by now," is his only comment.

Outside on the deck, several cats lie in the sun and a tame seagull, aptly named Tappy, walks about the plastic roof, tapping with its beak to show it wants to be fed.

"Collin trained it," explains Shendra, giving it a piece of muffin.

Sharie peers across the bay towards Edgecombe and Whitestone islands. "Don't some Arabs own those?"

"You mean the Aga Khan," says Shendra. "He sold Whitestone to Robin Williams, the film star."

Allen points out the small island where in 1958 he began building *Ocean Girl,* a forty-five-foot schooner and his biggest boat to date.

"We called it Oren Island, after the man who owned it then. He let me work there and in return I left him a lovely boat shed."

Back on *China Cloud,* Allen shows me the log he'd kept while he was building *Ocean Girl.* On June 15, 1958, two days after he'd begun work on the boat, he wrote, "Find it hard to get down to the old grind again. Every boat I build I say it will be the last, and I sure as hell hope it will be this time." Four days later, he wrote, "Not going to work such long hours, either. Get too tired and depressed." Beneath this entry, Sharie noted, "Where have I heard that before?"

Two and a half years later, *Ocean Girl* was launched. And by 1963 Allen was building his next boat, *Native Girl.*

J U L Y 9 ■ Barrie Farrell and his young Chinese wife, Lee, come to visit from Vancouver, bringing stacks of kindling and firewood for *China Cloud*'s stove. Barrie, a youthful sixty-year-old, is dressed in jeans and a checked shirt. He has Allen's hands and cornflower-blue eyes, and his fine, greying red hair is pulled back in a ponytail. There's a contemplative air about him, and he sits quietly on deck, saying little. He's also a boat builder, well known for the fibreglass boats with semi-displacement hulls that he's developed for the fishing industry. When I ask him if he's ever sailed, he smiles shyly and shakes his head. Later, however, when he and Lee have left, Allen tells me a story to the contrary.

In 1982, on the day *China Cloud* was due to be launched in Scottie Bay on Lasqueti Island, Sharie got an attack of glaucoma.

"At breakfast she couldn't eat her porridge or anything—she was really sick. So I beat it up to the phone and the doctor came and got the hovercraft to take us to hospital. By the time Barrie arrived for the launching, we were gone. He phoned the hospital, then he set off for Nanaimo on *Native Girl*—even though he'd never sailed before. It was blowing a southeaster out in Sabine Channel and he thought, God, I'll never get there tacking this way. He tried to start the engine, but smoke and sparks came out of it. I'd stopped using an engine by then, and it hadn't been run for ages. So he turned around and *sailed* back into Scottie Bay in a screaming southeaster, in the dark, with no experience!"

"It must be in the blood, Allen," I say.

He smiles. "Maybe it is."

*Echoes of the past
in Pender Harbour.*

J U L Y   1 0   ■   During the night it rains, but when morning comes the sun rapidly burns off the clouds, and steam rises from the rigging of *China Cloud*. Allen pours buckets of saltwater onto the decks and scrubs them down. Sharie moves around him, pegging out the clothes she's just washed along the rope railing. Dag, meanwhile, is off on some small islands close to Irvines Landing, photographing the old cabins there. When he comes back we all sit on the deck of *Luna Moth* and have lunch—bread, hardtack, cheese, lots of butter for Allen, apples and grapes.

"Those islands you went to this morning, we called them the Indian Islands," Allen tells Dag. "When I first came here a few Indian families lived at Irvines Landing. I remember watching them carve a dugout canoe from a big tree trunk. Then some white people wanted the land they were on, and moved them off to the islands. I knew the Julius family quite well. One Christmas Eve, the Union Steamship was leaving Irvines Landing for Vancouver, and the skipper was drunk. As he backed the ship out he let it drift too far and it crunched up on the rocks right next to the Julius's place, so close they could have reached out of their window and touched the stern. It was stuck until the tide came up the following morning."

"What happened to the Julius family?" Dag asks.

"I guess they went to the reserve in Sechelt. There used to be lots of Indian families living in shacks up and down the coast. But they're all gone. I don't know why. There used to be a lot of homesteaders around, too. You go into these old deserted places where the houses are rotting and falling down, and the orchards have got fruit on still and everything's overgrown—and you just feel so sad about all the lost dreams. So much work—beachcombing, clearing land, cutting trees, splitting shakes, hunting and fishing, salting and preserving, growing vegetables and storing them. People had their children there, but then it got too cold and exhausting, or maybe they were lonesome or sick or something. So they left and all their hard work got covered up by the bush."

The kettle is boiling merrily. I make herb tea for Allen, black tea for the rest of us, and pass around cookies. Outside one of the houses on shore, a man has appeared with a gas leafblower strapped to his back, and soon the peace is shattered by the whine of its engine.

"What's he doing?" asks Sharie.

She's dumbfounded by my explanation.

"What's wrong with a rake?"

■

"Want to go and see where we used to live?" asks Allen. We've hinted as much several times, but left the final decision to Allen. Since he and Sharie sold their property here forty-six years ago, they've often anchored in Bargain Harbour in their various boats, but have never been back to their old cabin.

The cabin in Bargain Harbour, seen from the water.

"We'd better ask Blanche first," he says.

Blanche Paton, an impeccably garbed and coiffed senior, now owns the property, which is adjacent to her large, modern, waterfront house. Her family uses the cabin as a summer home, and she assures us that little has been done to it since the Farrells left.

"How much did you pay for that five acres in 1939?" she asks Allen.

"A hundred and ninety dollars," he tells her. "It seemed like a fortune; I was only earning thirty dollars a month at the time. I sold it nine years later for eighteen hundred dollars—half for us and half for Betty."

"It would sell for at least half a million dollars today," says Blanche.

He shakes his head in wonder.

"Thank goodness I got rid of it in time. It would be awful to have so much money."

A pathway winds away from Blanche's house and through the trees. There's no sign of the cabin at first, but suddenly the foliage opens up to reveal it: the stone chimney stack that Allen built, the original shakes on the outside walls, the casement windows. Outside the cabin, a young robin hops around a bush of Saskatoon berries, eating his fill.

"Well, well," murmurs Allen. "Look at the old place."

He and Sharie linger for a minute in the low doorway, as if they're not quite ready to step into this part of their past.

"I built everything from stuff off the beaches and trees from the property," says Allen. "Except for the floor…we wanted it to be good for dancing on, so we bought fir and varnished it. On Saturday nights we filled the bathtub, put it in front of the fireplace and all had baths. We hauled the water by hand, from a spring a thousand feet away."

Finally we go inside. The room has heavy ceiling beams and an impressive stone fireplace. Doors lead to a kitchen and a bedroom the size of a closet. Allen built these two rooms first, and lived in them with his family while he finished the rest of the house. On the end wall of the living room is a steep staircase up to a loft, where Allen runs his hand over the walls.

"This is corrugated cardboard. I put it up and painted it white. It's lasted well."

Downstairs, Sharie sits gazing out of the window, lost in thought, with sunlight streaming over her shoulders.

"There used to be so many herring in the water you could scoop them up with your hands," she says, when I sit next to her. "When I first came here from Vancouver, I'd lie in bed and listen to all the fish. It sounded like rain. I thought it was wonderful."

"Ah, honey, back in time," sighs Allen.

Taking her hand, he leads her outside. We follow them along a path overgrown with ivy, down to the lagoon.

"Do you remember the lilac bushes, and the moon flowers that opened up at night?" he asks her on the way. "The lovely cabbages you grew, the apple trees and plum trees? Where have they gone?"

We sit on moss-covered rocks, staring down at the glittering water. No one speaks for a while. The air is heavy with nostalgia; Allen and Sharie are wrapped in memory. They began their long life together right here; they built *Wind Song,* their first sailing boat, along the shore of this lagoon. I shut my eyes, and lie back, feeling the sun's warmth bathe my face. I imagine the sound of Allen's saw as he makes planks for the boat, his children's laughter as they splash and swim nearby, and Sharie's musical voice as she calls to them that lunch is ready. Years roll away: the couple next to me are in their prime, strong and vigorous and full of plans, eager to fulfil their dreams.

"We had some wonderful times here," I hear Sharie say.

Allen's voice is quiet and sad. "We're on borrowed time, honey. There's so much more I want to do, I wish we could live another hundred years."

CHAPTER SEVEN

Nelson Island

JULY 11 ■ Helped by the ebbing tide, we sail out of Bargain Harbour around nine o'clock. Edgecombe Island slips by; ahead are the Whitestones, beyond them the imposing profile of Texada Island. It feels odd to be emerging from this tight little world and into the wide Strait of Georgia. Slowly, slowly, we get round Francis Point and cross the entrance to Pender Harbour. We've already had lunch by the time we're approaching the mouth of Agamemnon Channel, which leads around Nelson Island and up into Jervis Inlet. *China Cloud* left Bargain Harbour half an hour after us, and all morning we've managed to keep ahead of her, but now a westerly wind picks up, and she ploughs by. Allen is in the cockpit with a pencil and pad, sketching us. Next to him, Sharie holds the tiller.

"Isn't the scenery beautiful?" she calls over. Her face is alight; after all these years and all the sailing she's done, she's still brimming with appreciation for this coast.

With the sail set on a beam reach to catch the west wind, we head steadily north, along the wild shores of Nelson Island. The Farrells came this way together in 1952, after they returned from Fiji. The year before, on *Wind Song,* Allen had finally achieved his dream of sailing off to the South Seas. They reached Hawaii in twenty-six days, and from there spent another fifty-six days at sea before landing in Fiji. By then they were tired of sailing, and homesick. What their friend Dale Nordlund

Sailing into Blind Bay, Nelson Island.

calls the "big rubber band"—their attachment to the coast of B.C.—was already pulling them back. They sold *Wind Song* in Fiji and returned to Vancouver. In the basement of Sharie's mother's house, Allen built *Klee Wyck,* a fifteen-foot open boat, and they set off up the coast to look for land. After a week they reached Cape Cockburn, where now, forty-three years later, *China Cloud* sits in the sunshine, hove to and waiting for us.

"We stopped here in *Klee Wyck* and had a picnic," Allen calls over, as we catch up to him.

He leads the way round the cape, then lets go the sheet to slow his boat. Ahead of us are Kelly Island, Strawberry Island, Hardy Island; beyond them the steep, snow-capped mountains of Jervis Inlet. At the foot of bluffs along the shore of Nelson Island lie boulders of smooth, pale granite, rock that was mined here for years and now forms the base of the Parliament Buildings in Victoria, and of banks and courthouses all over Canada.

We're sailing closely beside *China Cloud,* propelled by a gentle evening breeze. Allen and Sharie are staring intently at the shore; although they've been back to Nelson Island many times since they sold their land in 1957, this is the first time since then that they've sailed in this way, past the property.

"The trees have grown so much," I hear Sharie say. "And these islands look bigger."

In golden evening light, we sail between Kelly Island and the small island they call Charman, and the land they once owned comes into sight.

"Our old place is up in the trees, behind that new house," calls Allen.

A man steps onto the deck of the house and takes a photo of *China Cloud*. Beyond him, on the beach, are the remains of a breakwater that I recognize from photographs in the Farrells' album. I turn to ask Allen if he'd like to go ashore here for a while, but he's already hauling in the sheet of his mainsail. *China Cloud* quickly picks up speed and bowls ahead, past some pretty little islands, and into Ballet Bay.

The small bay is named after the ballerina Audree Thomas. Her father, Harry Thomas, a one-armed First World War vet famed for his abilities as a sports fisherman, trapper and marksman, once owned the property around the bay. It offers good protection from northwest and southeast winds, and has lovely vistas across to Hardy Island and up towards Telescope Passage.

"We're safe here," says Allen, throwing fenders over the side so we can raft up. "And look—" he waves his arm to encompass islets and mountains and water "—isn't it beautiful?"

We're still tying up when a motorboat buzzes towards us.

"Hello, Grandpa and Grandma!" calls the young woman at the wheel, and the small child next to her waves excitedly.

Allen and Sharie peer uncertainly at Kari-Ann, their twenty-six-year-old granddaughter.

"You didn't recognize me because of my hair, eh?" she laughs.

"What happened to it?" asks Sharie in dismay. "It was so long and dark and lovely."

Kari-Ann runs a hand over her cropped, white-blonde tresses.

"Oh, I had it cut and dyed."

"God!" cries Allen. "Bloody hairdressers!"

Kari-Ann lives in Blind Bay, and when she saw *China Cloud* sailing past her house she immediately phoned the news to her father, Keray, who is the caretaker on Hardy Island, and her sister Lisa, over in

Westview, near Powell River. Tomorrow she's going shopping in Powell River, and she makes a list of things she can pick up for us.

"Good bread, nice and firm, with no molasses in it," says Sharie. "Butter. Soya milk. And some cold cuts of ham."

"With fat," adds Allen. "Lots of fat."

We request mosquito coils. Dag is convinced that the mosquitoes that come out every night to torment us are stowaways from the Fegan Islands, hiding by day in the dark corners of our boat.

"Coils?" repeats Kari-Ann in surprise. "I thought—seeing as you're travelling with Grandma and Grandpa—well, I figured you'd be environmentalists."

"We are," Dag assures her. "But please buy us some mosquito coils anyway, the more potent the better."

Allen and Sharie stay up longer than usual, and watch the sunset. The surrounding islands turn black, and the tops of their trees make a jagged silhouette against a darkening blue-gold sky.

"I think this is the best place on the coast," says Allen. "If we get sick and tired in Mexico, perhaps we'll come back, and build a little float house here. What do you think, honey?"

I glance at Sharie. She's smiling, but she doesn't look the least bit surprised.

When the moon rises, it's full and bright enough for us to read by. Dag wafts incense sticks around under our canopy, and the mosquitoes retreat for a while. We stretch out, rocked very gently by the boat. From the main cabin of *China Cloud* I hear Mario mewing and Sharie soothing him with quiet words, and I feel ridiculously happy, and completely content.

JULY 12 ■ This is the west coast at its finest: eagles wheeling beneath a clear blue sky, the air smelling of dry pine, the ocean warm and clear. We swim over to some smooth rocks, haul out and lie in the sun like a pair of seals. Presently a rough-hewn wooden boat, *Kari-Isle*, chugs into the bay and rafts up to the starboard side of *China Cloud*.

"Hey you guys, come and meet Keray!" calls Allen, and we swim back and sit with them on deck.

Over the last few weeks Allen and Sharie have told us lots of stories from Keray's childhood: the night he left *Wind Song* and went to shore

Allen tells Keray his plans to give away China Cloud.

across a boom stick, balancing himself with a branch, like a tightrope walker; the time he asked them to drop him off on an uninhabited island, where he built an outrigger canoe from driftwood and paddled back on his own; the impromptu song and dance shows with which he entertained them during their long voyage to the South Seas. At fifty-three, Keray is still boyish and ebullient, and seems cheerfully irreverent. He tells us about attending the Ballet Bay school, which opened in 1950 and was housed in a Quonset hut in the woods. He and his thirteen or so fellow pupils were delivered to the school each day by Lorne Maynard, a one-legged First World War veteran, who did a school run in a twenty-four-foot motor cruiser from Blind Bay and up through Jervis Inlet. In the four years Keray attended the school, there was a steady turnover of teachers.

"One of them used to eat her sandwiches while she was looking over our shoulders at our work, and drop crumbs down our backs," he recalls. "She rolled her own cigarettes in class, and she'd be spitting out tobacco even while she was strapping me. She strapped me for drawing boats instead of doing my arithmetic. Hell, if it wasn't for her, I could have been a naval architect by now!"

Clam digging on Nelson Island.

Hanging in the main cabin of *China Cloud* is Allen's painting of *Tiger Lily,* a pretty junk-rigged boat that Keray owned for a while in the seventies.

"When I first bought her, Dad thought she was a load of garbage. But I could take out the whole family, land the boat on a beach, step off and go clam-digging, step back on to feed the dog and Kari-Ann's duck, go and dig more clams, then float off with the tide. Pretty soon, Dad got to thinking about junks himself."

This is the first time he's seen Allen and Sharie since receiving their letter with the news that they are giving up *China Cloud.*

"I hope you're getting a good price for her," he says.

"Price? There's no price," Allen tells him. "We're giving her away."

Keray rolls his eyes, turns his baseball cap backwards, and paces the few steps from one side of *China Cloud*'s deck to the other.

"Well, Dad," he says, when he's regained his composure, "it's a good thing you're not giving the boat to me. I couldn't live up to the legend.

All these people that see *China Cloud* and come over to talk, I'd stick my head out of the hatch and yell at them, 'F— off!'"

Our laughter rouses Mario, who has been peacefully sleeping on a sack of bark in the small midship hold.

"What's happening to the cat when you give the boat away?" asks Keray, leaning down to stroke him.

"We thought you might like to have him," says Sharie. "I don't know how he'll do in your house, though. He's never lived on the land."

"He'll be fine with me, Mum," Keray reassures her. "And Tex will soon get used to him."

Tex is the large, black dog lying in the cabin of *Kari-Isle*. He seems quite amiable until Allen decides to have a look around the boat and steps onto the gunwale. Barking ferociously, Tex flies at him, hackles up and teeth bared. Mario leaps out of the hold and shoots down the companionway at a speed I never thought him capable of.

"Holy smokes," mutters Dag. "He'll get eaten alive."

At a word from Keray, the dog calms.

"Just look at that," says Allen, showing us the wet marks on his sleeve where Tex grabbed him. "He was really gentle, it was just a warning. You've trained him well, Keray."

He turns to Sharie, who has turned pale and is looking horror-struck.

"No one will hurt Mario with Tex around, honey. You don't have to worry."

JULY 13 ■ Four generations of Farrells sit in the sun on the deck of *China Cloud*. Kari-Ann has arrived with groceries for Allen and Sharie, and mosquito coils for us. Her daughter Lilian is clutching a cloth doll, stuffed with straw and dressed South Sea Island–style, that Allen made for Kari-Ann when she was a child. And Keray has brought a model of *China Cloud* that Allen gave him some years back. It's a perfect replica, but the rigging is tangled and broken in places, and needs replacing.

"I'll fix it straightaway," says Allen. "We won't leave until it's finished."

Lilian leaps into the water, and happily paddles round in circles, kept afloat by her life jacket.

"Look at me Grandpa!" she cries, and both Allen and Keray turn towards her.

"I can't get used to you being a grandfather," Allen tells Keray, shaking his head. "You're still just a kid!"

In the afternoon we accompany Allen and Sharie through the maze of small islands across from Ballet Bay to a place where they used to dig for clams. The tide is low, and a bar of white sand is exposed between two islands, forming a lagoon of jewel-green water. Sharie stays in the dory while the rest of us clamber onto the beach and start digging. Allen has brought a potato fork, and we take turns with it, making holes, then scrabbling through the wet sand with our fingers.

"The clams are in different layers," Allen tells me. "Soft shells on the top, then manilas—they're the best—then littlenecks, butter clams and horse clams."

I enjoy the feel of the damp sand between my fingers, the sun on my back, the triumph when I pull out a large, live clam.

"It's not so much fun in winter," Allen reminds me.

When we return to the dory with a string sack bulging with shells, Sharie sniffs the air appreciatively. "Mmmm, a nice clammy smell."

On *China Cloud*, Allen shucks the clams, Dag chops them finely, and I help Sharie make them into patties. While we work, Allen reminisces about the community events he and Sharie attended on Nelson Island, back in the fifties.

"About once a month there was a dance at the quarry dining hall near Blind Bay. You'd get fifty or so people there, dancing to gramophone records or to musicians playing squeeze box and guitar. Anyone who didn't want to fight left by midnight."

In their album there's a photograph of him dressed as a cowboy on a horse for a Hallowe'en dance.

"I won first prize! The legs were stuffed with straw and the hooves were wooden. I could clomp over the floor and rear up. We put the horse through something that night, and by the next day the legs had lost all their stuffing. Another time I went as a woman. I had makeup on, a blouse with grapefruits up it, a skirt and woollen stockings that kept falling down. When I got out of the boat at the float all the dogs started barking at me!"

On one of the island sports days, Allen won all the events.

Allen building "Farrell's Folly," the breakwater in Blind Bay, Nelson Island, 1957.

"The egg and spoon race, the sack race, the nail-driving race, the wheelbarrow race—I was forty years old and there were all these twenty-year-old loggers and I beat them all!"

J U L Y   1 4   ■   Allen claims he's too busy working on Keray's model to visit his old property on Blind Bay, close to Kelly and Charman islands, and tells us to go without him and Sharie. We're greeted there by a tall, strongly built man with a neatly clipped moustache, who introduces himself as Colonel Pond.

"I've been made an honorary general," he adds briskly, "so you can call me Colonel or General, whichever you prefer."

Although in his seventies, the colonel has only recently retired from the American Air Force, and still works as a military historian for the California State Museum. He and his wife have been spending their summers in Blind Bay for many years.

"After we'd bought this place I met Allen Farrell in Pender Harbour," he recalls. "He was working with an adze on a piece of wood

Allen on Grey Gull *in Blind Bay, Nelson Island, 1956.*

and I stopped to introduce myself. I said something like 'Hello, I'm Colonel Bill Pond,' and he walked away and ignored me."

I suppress a smile at the thought of Allen, with his strong pacifist beliefs, finding himself faced with a dyed-in-the-wool military man.

"Perhaps he didn't hear you," I tactfully suggest.

"Perhaps not. Please tell him from me that we've done all we can to preserve his work around here."

Following the colonel around the ten-acre property, the realization of what Allen and Sharie achieved here in just over four years begins to sink in. In addition to Allen working at various jobs to make a living, he and Sharie cleared land, felled trees, created a garden, renovated *Klee Wyck,* built a thirty-foot sailing boat and other smaller boats, and more.

Their garden is now overgrown, and there's no sign of the grape arbour they told us about, or the sixteen fruit trees they planted. But their two-room cabin, the tiny log house they built for Keray, the woodshed, and the huge cedar shake deer fence are all still in good repair.

Dag gazes in astonishment at the eight-foot fence. "It's simple and functional, but beautiful as well," he says, "like everything else they create."

Down on the beach, we inspect Allen's breakwater. He began it after he returned from a trip to England, where he was inspired by the rock-work in the harbours there. Known locally as "Farrell's Folly," it would have been eighty feet long, fifteen feet wide at the base and eighteen feet high, had he stayed to finish it.

As much as he and Sharie loved this property, the land couldn't hold Allen. At the water's edge are the remains of a steam box. And standing on pilings is the boat shed where he made *Klee Wyck* into *Grey Gull;* built the thirty-foot *Ocean Bird,* a boat rigged with a gaff sail and two foresails; built two sixteen-foot outboard boats and one double-ended rowboat; and did many repair jobs for local people. Stepping carefully over the rotting timbers, we read some notes pencilled in Allen's familiar handwriting onto one of the supporting posts.

Sunday	2	nails $10
Mon	5	copper paint $1.00
Tue	7	green paint $1.00
Wed	7	
Thurs	5	
Keray	2 $1/2$	

"Most people couldn't build a boat like *Ocean Bird* in four years," says Dag wonderingly, "never mind everything else they did at the same time."

Before we leave, the colonel shows us the remains of a weir where native peoples once fished during summer months. The fish would drift towards the shore on the rising tide, swim over the weir and become trapped behind it when the tide ebbed.

"And look," Pond points to a shallow, smooth depression in a near-by boulder, "while the guys were standing behind the weir, spearing the fish, their gals would sit here and grind clam shells to make powder for painting their faces with, and cornmeal to eat."

Recently, when some members of the Sechelt First Nation came to look at the weir, he asked them to give his property a name in their language.

"They called it something that means 'The Big Chief Lives Here,'" says the Colonel, looking very proud.

Over supper, we tell the Farrells about our visit to their old property.

"It's a great spot," says Dag. "Protected from the northeast and southwest winds, beautiful views."

"Oh, I loved it there," sighs Sharie. "I wasn't ready to leave that little house."

"Why did you leave so soon?" I ask.

She shrugs and smiles; it's Allen who answers.

"When we finished *Ocean Bird* we moved aboard for a little while, then we decided to stay on her. Well, I decided—much to Sharie's disgust. But if we'd stayed, I would have started building a stone house like the ones I saw in England. I had it all planned."

"That's right," she laughs. "Thank goodness we left in time."

J U L Y   1 5   ■   A family of otters is making a commotion along the shore, splashing about excitedly, running back and forth over a rock. Dag goes to investigate, then calls me over. Lying on the rock is a wolf eel, about six feet long. Its graceful, tapering body is topped by a monstrous head with ferocious-looking jaws, a visage not improved by the otters, who have chewed through its cheeks.

"I wonder what wolf eel tastes like?" Dag ponders, then unclips his knife from his belt and cuts off a large fillet from the creature's side. "We'll have this for lunch."

A shoal of little shiner perch have taken to hanging round our rudder, eagerly awaiting the leftovers we throw into the water at mealtimes. Since arriving in Ballet Bay we've discovered that perch are ambivalent about pasta, but adore couscous; they treat bits of chopped-up onion with disdain, leaving them to float down into the shadowy depths, yet they fight over raw garlic. This morning I threw them the rest of our sourdough pancake steeped in maple syrup, which, after the first few exploratory nibbles, they devoured. But after lunch all we can offer them are a few grains of rice, for Dag's curried wolf eel was delicious, and we've eaten every scrap.

Allen spends all day restoring Keray's model. When the fine details of this work give him eyestrain, he has a break and comes up from the cabin to sit in the sun and chat to us. But he can't rest: within minutes he's re-caulking part of the deck. Presently a helicopter flies in from the south. It circles above Ballet Bay, drops towards us, then settles on the dock outside the only summer home along the shoreline. The blades continue to whirr as two men jump out and run along the dock and up to the house. Soon they reappear carrying a heavy bag between them. Once they're aboard, the helicopter lifts off, hovering above the water like a giant bug. People on the dozen or so other boats anchored in the bay stand on their decks, curiously watching the helicopter. For a few seconds it hangs in the air directly above *China Cloud,* while the men in its glass bubble peer down at the junk. The engine noise is deafening, and the wind from its blades blows Allen's hair into his eyes. But he continues caulking, completely ignoring the presence of the helicopter, acting as if it simply doesn't exist.

J U L Y   1 6   ■   Visiting *China Cloud* for the morning are Cliff and Susan Foreman, who were part of the artists' community in Irvines Landing, Pender Harbour, when they first met the Farrells in 1967.

"They were anchored close by in *Native Girl.* Every day we'd see Allen jogging past our place on his way for a run up and down Pender Hill," Cliff laughs. "How old were you then, Allen? Fifty-something? We were all in our twenties and it was far more than any of us could do."

For the last twenty-three years, Cliff and Susan have lived on Nelson Island, in Hidden Basin. This bottle-shaped inlet is a difficult place to access. Its narrow entrance has treacherous tidal currents, and its northern side can only be reached by foot, along woodland paths. They invite us to visit them, and give us directions to their house which include crossing a creek, climbing over fallen trees, taking one turn at an enormous tree, another at a hen house.

In the afternoon we set off for Hidden Basin. As we trek through the forest, Allen shows us how to identify different trees: balsam, fir, hemlock, wild cherry, alder, yew, cedar. Spreading ferns grow between them, mosses creep up their trunks, witches'-hair lichen hangs from their branches. Along the paths are ripening Oregon grape and salal berries, thimble berries and huckleberries.

"I remember once rowing around at this time of year and seeing the shore all red," says Allen. "I didn't know what it was until I got close to the bushes loaded with huckleberries. The black huckleberries get ripe in September. In winter I used to pick the branches and take them over to Pender Harbour. They were shipped from there to Vancouver and sold to florists. I'd be out in the pouring rain, with Keray under one arm and a bundle of black huck under the other, sliding down steep slopes."

For Sharie, the path is made hazardous by roots, rocks and fallen trees, but she gamely tackles everything and never complains. At last we step out of the shade of the woods and onto a sunlit bluff. The air is hot and still. A haze rises from the turquoise water of Hidden Basin. There are no boats at anchor, no houses in sight around its shores. The silence is broken only by birdsong.

"I used to come here often to visit my good friend Florence," says Sharie quietly. "It's so strange to think that she's not around anymore."

The two women met in Vancouver when Sharie was working as a secretary and Florence was a broadcaster with CBC radio. One summer Florence and her brother went on a trip up the coast. They reached Hidden Basin, or Hidden Bay as it was then known. It reminded them of the place where they grew up in Nova Scotia, and Florence became enamoured with a waterfront property. Back in Vancouver she contacted the Lands Office and discovered that the property was owned by Frederick Frederickson, a well-known radiologist, who was installing some of the first x-ray machines in Vancouver hospitals. She went to see him at his office, hoping to persuade him to sell the land. Outside his door she twice lost her nerve and nearly turned back. Finally, she plucked up courage and knocked. Frederick was later to recount that he looked into her eyes and fell in love immediately. He offered her the lease of the land for a dollar a year, and asked her out on a date.

"The problem was her boyfriend," says Sharie. "He lived on a boat, the *Escapade*. He was a real military type."

Florence's boyfriend didn't take kindly to her affair with Frederickson, and hired a private detective to trail her and her friends, including Sharie. Eventually, when the fuss died down, Florence and Freddie were married, and lived on a float house in Vancouver. In the fifties, when Freddie retired, they moved to Hidden Basin. For a while

Dale Nordlund

Allen and Sharie caulking the deck of Ocean Bird, *1958.*

Florence was the postmistress, working out of the little post office in Billings Bay. Freddie died about twelve years ago, but Florence lived on until 1993.

"We were the same age," says Sharie wistfully. "She was out raking leaves, and she just keeled over, and was gone."

As we follow a path along the bluff, I imagine for a second that I see a turret among the trees. I blink, and look again. There *is* a turret, and below it a roof with sweeping Japanese lines. On the beach, at the foot of a steep cliff, is an edifice built from scrap plywood and beachcombed logs. This is the home of Ralph Payne, who comes out to meet us. He has known Allen and Sharie since 1958, when they were building *Ocean Girl* on Oren's Island and he was an eleven-year-old living in Pender Harbour. Curious about the couple and their boat, Ralph and a friend rolled a log off the beach in Bargain Harbour, sat astride it and paddled it with a couple of sticks the two miles or so out to Oren's Island. Such determination followed Ralph into adulthood. His slight frame and

Riding the currents in Skookumchuck Narrows.

monkish demeanour belie the effort that went into creating his home, or the demands of living in such an isolated place. He began building the house in 1980, half a mile away along the bay. A year later he floated it on logs to its present site, on Crown land, because it offered better soil and water. Since then he has invested it with much hard work and love; more than a home, it is a haven for him, where his creativity and spirituality can flourish. I ask him what would happen if anyone objected to him being on this land.

"Me and the house have grown roots here over the past fifteen years," he says. "It would be hard to move and start over somewhere else. And the whole coast is developing so fast. Where could I go?"

"It used to be easy to be a squatter," Allen tells him. "You found a nice spot, collected some wood, built a shack. No one complained. God! These days people make you feel uncomfortable if all you're doing is picking bark off the beach in front of their place."

"I don't think anyone should own property," says Ralph, with a quiet vehemence, "and if they do, it should revert back to the Crown when they die."

He shows us around his house. A large workshop on the first floor is stuffed with equipment for his wood-working and wood-turning projects. Beneath the windows, nettles sprout from planters made from oil drums, and lettuce and pepper plants are flourishing on the deck outside. From the workshop he takes us through a small tidy kitchen, with a ceiling supported by bark-covered logs, and up a spiral wooden staircase to the first floor of the turret.

A large desk follows the curve of the walls, a coil of fat rope serves as a mat on the painted plywood floor, plastic crates set on their sides hold meticulously arranged books. Sunlight is streaming through the windows; the room is bright and warm. I can imagine spending days here alone, reading and thinking, gazing out along the bay, relishing the quiet and the solitude.

"It's wonderful in the summer," Ralph agrees. "But in the winter, when it rains for weeks on end—well, then I wish I had someone to share this place with."

Cliff and Susan, who live fifteen minutes' walk from Ralph, seem a little startled when Dag and I turn up at their door later in the day, as if they didn't expect we'd make the effort to get here. Not many people casually drop in, and Cliff and Susan rarely leave. Tied up to the float below their house are a thirty-five-foot steel boat, which Cliff tells us is good for when the bay is iced up, and a nineteen-foot runabout. Neither boat has a working engine at the moment, so when Susan and Cliff need to get across to Saltery Bay to pick up mail, or Powell River to shop, they go through the woods to Blind Bay and hitch a ride with Allen's granddaughter Kari-Ann and her partner, Tony. It's an isolation I can't imagine, but they have had time to grow used to it. Susan home-schooled their four children, two of whom still live with her and Cliff.

"It's lonely sometimes," she admits. "When Florence Frederickson was alive she had some of her trees cut down just so that she could see our lights at night across the bay."

After twenty years of being constrained by tidal currents, Cliff is working on an easier way to get out of Hidden Basin. Proudly, he

unrolls a set of plans, and shows us the drawings for the vessel he's planning to start building soon—a hovercraft.

"With this," he says, his eyes gleaming, "we'll be able to leave *whenever* we feel like it."

J U L Y   1 7   ■   Ralph Payne arrives in his small motorboat to take us
to Cape Cockburn, where his old friend Harry Roberts lived. The
Farrells also knew Harry well, but they're expecting visitors today, so
can't come with us. They chuckle at their memories of him. Harry was
a colourful, controversial character, strong of mind and opinions, but
with a big heart.

"He came to see us when we were building *Wind Song,*" says Sharie.
"He kept talking for hours, telling all sorts of stories. Allen really wanted to get back to work on the boat but he was too polite to say so. He
just gritted his teeth and listened. Finally Harry left, and a few days later
we got a letter from him apologizing for taking up so much of our time
and sending a five-dollar bill towards the boat—five dollars was a lot of
money in those days!"

Roberts came from England to British Columbia in 1900, when he
was sixteen years old. His grandparents had homesteaded near Sechelt,
and when they moved down to Vancouver, members of the Sechelt First
Nation presented them with a "white man's" dugout canoe, adapted for
oars instead of paddles. It was in this boat that Harry, his father and two
siblings rowed the thirty or so miles from Vancouver up to the family
property. For almost three decades, Roberts was a key figure in developing the settlement at what became known as Roberts Creek. He
established a store and a sawmill, he worked as postmaster, rowing out
in a skiff in all weathers to collect mail from the passing Union
Steamships, and he served as a justice of the peace. He also built many
boats, of all descriptions. His first sailing boat was a thirty-six-foot yawl,
named *Odamit* after the oath Roberts often uttered during its construction. Later the name was changed to *Chack Chack,* a native word
meaning "bald eagle." Roberts, who was balding himself by then,
became known as Skipper Chack Chack. He finished his second sailing
boat, *Leyo,* in the early thirties, shortly before he moved to Nelson
Island and began homesteading on Cape Cockburn.

Ralph ties up his boat in Cockburn Bay, and we slog under scorching sunshine along dusty logging roads. Our efforts are rewarded by a sublime crescent beach, covered with pebbles as smooth as birds' eggs, and strewn with huge heaps of bleached logs. The ocean is calm and lambent, irresistible after our hot, sweaty walk. But when I strip off and run in, ice-cold water seizes me. Gasping with shock, I struggle back to shore.

"You were too fast for me to warn you," says Ralph sympathetically. "There are big upwellings here; the water is always freezing."

Sunray, Roberts's fabled log house, stands on a grassy point at the far end of the beach. He built it low to the ground to withstand the battering of winter winds and installed seventeen large windows, with panes cut and separated by cedar strips to resemble rays of light. Roberts shared Sunray with two different wives, three children and many friends and visitors. It was his home until the mid-seventies, when he could no longer look after himself. He was carried along the trail to Hidden Basin, where Florence Frederickson cared for him until he died, aged ninety-five. Roberts was a resident of Nelson Island for forty-seven years, longer than anyone else in its recorded history. He, his house and boats were renowned all along the coast. Sadly, after his passing, vandals smashed in his unique windows. On the beach in front of the house lie the rotting remains of his last boat, the thirty-five-foot, two-masted *Chack Chack 3*. It was never launched, and now it's only a shell, gradually being colonized by sea grasses.

Ralph has brought with him a copy of "The Natural Laws of Chack Chack," a pamphlet written by Roberts in which he outlines his philosophies. I page through it, reading his opinions about the cause of society's ills: that people try to achieve happiness through material things, instead of living more simply and using their creative abilities to gain personal satisfaction.

"He writes that people overeat and fill their houses with clutter that gives them no satisfaction," I tell Dag. "And that in creative accomplishments we should use our hands as well as our heads."

"Sounds like something Allen might say," he comments.

As we walk around Sunray, it strikes me that Harry Roberts had a great deal in common with Allen—he was a boatbuilder and a painter, a man who worked with the natural materials in his environment and

After all these years, Sharie and Ann Pettigrew finally meet.

who combined artistic genius with practicality. The house is on five different levels, and appears to have grown with the whims and moods of
its creator, rather than being consciously designed. In the large main
room, the cement floor is painted red, blue and yellow to look like
colourful irregular tiles. The mantlepiece of the huge stone fireplace is
inscribed "1938." Glass bottles set in the cement act as tiny windows.
Some have been broken, and above them vines are creeping through
between the wall and roof. A sign put up by the caretakers of the house,
who leave it open for all comers, asks us to "Please respect Harry's
memory. Leave no garbage, light no fires. Enjoy the peace and quiet.
Take only pictures."

We wander up to a galley area above the main room, in and out of
bedrooms, a larder, a kitchen and a little bathroom. From the back porch
we gaze out on Roberts's old garden, and his orchards where plums and
Transparent apples are ripening. Along one wall of the house, log pony
walls create little nooks, each lit by a window. A photograph of Harry
taken in his last years shows him sitting in the nook beneath where his
image now hangs, next to one of his sunbeam windows. He looks content, and I imagine him calmly facing death after a long and full life.

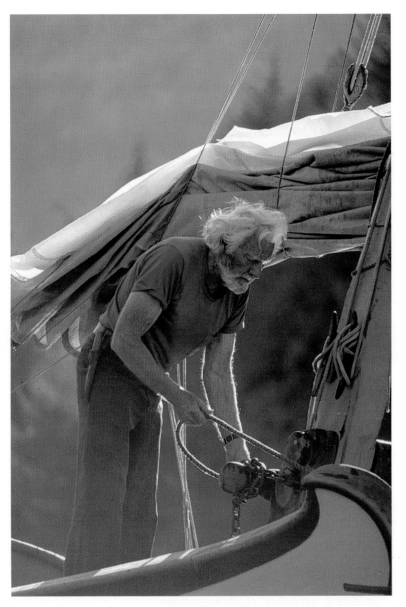

At the end of a long day's sail, Allen adjusts the anchor warp.

Evening over Snake Island.

China Cloud *and* Luna Moth *becalmed.*

Bill Wilkinson ponders the work still needed on his replica of China Cloud.

Jimmy Dougan's homestead in Whitaker Bay, Texada Island.

Net loft in Pender Harbour.

Dwarfed by a fir, behind Jimmy's homestead.

Whiskey Slough,
Pender Harbour.

Luna Moth *rafted up to* China Cloud *in Ballet Bay.*

Harry Roberts's homestead on Cape Cockburn, Nelson Island.

Finn Bay.

Running with the wind into Desolation Sound.

Allen's trademark blend of beauty and functionality.

Cruising through Waddington Channel in Desolation Sound.

Last days on China Cloud.

Ralph, who knew Roberts and helped him look after Sunray during his final years there, quickly puts paid to my illusion. He describes how Roberts often sat beneath an apple tree in Florence Frederickson's garden, with photos and plans of the houses and boats he'd built spread over a table before him.

"He still held to his ideas of Natural Law," he says, "and at the end he was always trying to convince himself that his role in life had been worthwhile, and justifiable in the eyes of the Creator."

JULY 18   ■   Ann Pettigrew, who worked as Harry Roberts's housekeeper during the forties, now lives alone on an eight-acre island, across from Ballet Bay. Sharie is intrigued to think that a woman older than herself, albeit by only a year, is managing to live in such a remote place, and she's keen to pay Ann a visit.

Around ten o'clock, with the temperature climbing towards the high seventies, we row over to Ann's Island. As we approach the beach, she emerges from the trees. Stepping carefully over logs, she comes down to the water's edge, waving to us with both hands.

"I've been looking at your boat for days," she loudly tells Sharie as we climb out of the dory. "We've never met, but I heard all about you when you lived in Blind Bay."

"Did you? Oh dear," laughs Sharie.

Ann turns to me. "I can't hear a thing, so you can be my interpreter. Shout in my ear and tell me what everyone says."

Ann is robust for eighty-nine. Her cheeks are plump and her skin is soft, clear and astonishingly unwrinkled. Fine, grey-blond hair is pulled back from her face with an Alice band and tied into two braids that fall to her waist.

"My hair used to be so long I could sit on it," she tells me, as we walk up the path, "but this is all that's left."

The Farrells are enchanted by her cabin, a tiny old place covered with cedar shakes. The island is free of deer, and around the cabin irises and lilies bloom in pots, planters and a rockery. Lily of the valley, rare ferns and succulents peek out between the roots of tall trees. An enamel bowl is mounted on a stand for a bird bath, a Raccoon Restaurant sign hangs from the eaves of the cabin, and in the trees high above it, tame squirrels madly chase each other, making gymnastic leaps from branch to branch.

Ann tells us that a fisherman called Tom Hughes had the cabin towed here after the war. He had acquired this island under the home-site lease being offered to fishermen at the time.

"For years he'd been going by in his boat. He said the sun shines here more than anywhere else in the bay, so he decided this was where he wanted to live. It used to be called Tom's Island while he was alive."

While she was working at Sunray, Ann became friends with Tom, and used to visit him here after she moved to West Vancouver. When Tom died, he willed the island to Ann and her daughter.

"We had a mission boat in those days and when Tom was really bad, Reverend Green asked him what he was going to do about the island. Tom said he hadn't made any arrangements, so the Reverend said, 'Why not leave it to the girls?'—that was me and Jacquie. 'Do you think they could manage it?' said Tom. 'I think they'd give it their best!' said the Reverend. He had some papers drawn up and brought them to Tom to sign. But he was too weak to write—all he could manage was an X, and Reverend Green signed it as a witness. After he died, we weren't sure if it would be legal, but it worked out fine. I haven't changed the island in forty years; it's just as it was when Tom was alive."

Hearing a whining and scratching behind the cabin door, I lean over and shout in Ann's ear, "I think there's a dog inside."

"Oh, poor Daisy, I locked her in," she says, opening the door just wide enough to release a white, broad-beamed cocker spaniel. It wriggles around her feet, clutching a sock in its mouth, then hurries down the steps and disappears into some salal bushes.

"There are socks of mine all over this island," says Ann resignedly.

She invites us to stay for tea, and leads us along a path through the woods to the deck of a much newer house which belongs to her son-in-law, Geoffrey Partington. He married Jacquie Pettigrew aboard the coast mission boat *John Antler* in 1959, and they honeymooned here on the island. Last year, Ann tells us, her daughter died. She sighs sadly, then takes my arm.

"Now that everyone's settled, you can come back with me, and help make the tea."

Jervis Inlet.

Halfway back to her cabin, she stops and points to a small trail leading off into the woods.

"I'll go and put the kettle on," she says, "while you look at the
graves."

Graves? I stare after her and Daisy until the path bends and takes
them out of sight. Then, hesitantly, I set off along the trail. In a clearing
among the trees, dappled by sunlight shafting through the forest canopy,
are two long, low mounds of earth. One has a granite headstone, simply inscribed: Thomas Hughes 1885–1956. The other, unmarked and
more recently dug, has pots filled with nasturtiums and pansies set
around it. A couple of butterflies are lightly moving from flower to
flower. I've always felt uneasy in graveyards, unable to make any con-
nection between the earth I'm standing on and the person buried
beneath it. But here I feel relaxed, and at peace. I sit next to the
unmarked grave, and close my eyes. The air is filled with the whirring
of crickets. A breeze rustles through the foliage, carrying with it the
smell of salt and dry cedar. From above the trees, a bald eagle makes its
creaky call, *kleek-kik-ik-ik-ik,* and close by a woodpecker starts drilling

on a tree trunk. I think about the old fisherman lying beneath me: could he have guessed, when he first saw this island from his boat, that one day he would become part of it? And I think of how perfect this place is, that there could be nowhere better than this to end one's days.

■

The cabin is stuffed with years of possessions —clothes spill out of cardboard boxes and plastic bags, papers are piled high, bric-a-brac covers every surface, a lovebird hops around a cage. Ann is bent over the sink, sorting through a pile of dishes. When I touch her shoulder she turns and says, "Did you see the graves? Jacquie's stone isn't there yet."

While we set trays and search around for packets of cookies, Ann tells me about herself.

"I lived in Vancouver as a child, and then the Fraser Valley, but every summer my family took the steamships and went camping up along the coast."

At the start of this century, camping holidays became very popular, reaching a peak between 1912 and 1920. The Union Steamship lines put on extra boats at weekends, and the six o'clock Friday-night run was known as the "Daddy Special" because of all the working men who were travelling from the city to meet their vacationing families.

"We'd stop off in places like Garden Bay, in Pender Harbour. We camped on the Indian reserve there, and I remember watching the bears come in to eat the kinnikinnick. Do you know what that is? It's a shrub that the Indians used as tobacco. I've got some growing here, I'll show you on the way back."

Ann was married for a while, had her daughter and then got one of the first legal separations in B.C. She worked as a nanny in Vancouver, and then, in 1942, was offered the job of housekeeper at Sunray, after Harry Roberts's second wife left him and their three children.

"I moved up with my daughter, our dog, goats, rabbits, all our belongings. I didn't want to be called mother. My real name is Edie, but that didn't sound appropriate for the children either. So they decided to call me Ann, and it's stuck ever since."

When I ask her what it was like working for Harry, she laughs.

"Oh, it was hard sometimes. I was teaching all the children through correspondence. Harry was no help with their education, he thought things like algebra were of no use. I had to look after the house as well, and work in the garden. There was rationing, so we mostly ate vegetables and rabbits. I stuck it out for four years—I had no choice. It was the war, what else could I do? Then I got sick and had to go to the city for an operation. I wasn't so strong after that, and Harry didn't want me back."

She and Jacquie settled in West Vancouver, on five acres of land. When Jacquie was married and moved to Vancouver Island, Ann lived with her for part of each year. They spent many summers on the island they inherited, but it's only recently that Ann has come to live here full time. And soon she faces a winter in a cabin without electricity or running water.

"But there's different kinds of uncomfortableness," she tells me, as we walk back through the woods. "To me, being stuck in a city rest home would be horrific."

Back at her son-in-law's house, we find Allen in a restless mood.

"I stood in some of that dog's shit," he says, as Ann passes round cups of tea and plates of shortbread cookies. "It's all over my feet."

"What did he say?" asks Ann.

Sharie looks radiant. She and Ann constantly exchange smiles, and lean towards each other, shouting into each other's ears. Allen, however, keeps glancing at his watch.

"It's twenty to twelve!" he finally exclaims. "Nearly lunchtime! Come on, honey, we've got to go!"

"Not yet, honey," Sharie cajoles. "We've just eaten all these lovely cookies. I'm not hungry."

But he's already helping her to her feet. As we walk back to the beach, Ann takes my arm.

"Harry Roberts was an original, you know," she says confidentially. "And originals are inspiring, but they can sometimes be difficult."

J U L Y 1 9 ■ Dag and I are going to Vancouver for three days to take part in a BBC TV documentary, an arrangement made long ago. Allen and Sharie insist they don't mind us interrupting the trip. In our absence they'll start sorting out their belongings. They want the boat to be empty when they hand her over to Gerry, and all they plan to take to Mexico are a change of clothes, their Spanish grammar book, Allen's paints and a few medicines.

At three o'clock, a float plane lands in Ballet Bay and picks us up from the dock belonging to the summer house. Within minutes, *China Cloud* and *Luna Moth* are tiny dots amidst a huge, resplendent landscape of ocean and islands and mountains. Half an hour later, we descend into the city, and another world. As we walk towards a taxi rank, people glance at us wonderingly. Our hair, washed in the ocean for the past few weeks, looks like straw; we're brown as berries and dressed in rumpled, salt-stained clothes. And Dag, of course, is barefoot. It occurs to me that he won't be allowed through the doors of the hotel where we have reservations. When a taxi draws up, we quickly slide into the back seat.

"Where to?" asks the driver.

"A shoe store," we tell him.

CHAPTER EIGHT

Van Anda and Lund

JULY 22 ■ As the plane circles down over Ballet Bay, the Farrells stand on the deck of *China Cloud,* waving to us. Soon, we're sitting across the table from them once more, sharing tea and cookies and laughter. But something has changed in our absence. Most of the ornaments are gone, and the shelves behind the benches are empty. Mario, at least, is still here. Allen and Sharie have decided to keep him until our trip together is over, then drop him off with Keray on their way south.

"Poor Mario," murmurs Sharie, lifting him onto her lap. "We don't know what's ahead, do we puss?"

Over lunch Allen looks at charts, pointing out anchorages we could pull into on our way to Desolation Sound.

"I promised I'd visit Terrible Ted on Texada Island, to look at a boat he's building. Maybe we'll go there if the wind is right."

"*Terrible* Ted?"

"I don't know why he's called that," says Allen, "except maybe for how he's built."

Around four o'clock, a southeasterly blows up. Two hours later, we tack into Maude Bay, on the north shore of the mouth of Jervis Inlet. Behind the summer cabins lining the bay is abandoned farmland where, in past summers, Allen and Sharie have picked pounds of blackberries and blackcaps. But none of us feels like going ashore this evening. We raft up, and Dag and I make dinner with groceries we brought back with us: barbecued chicken, salads, gooseberries and cream. When we've eaten, Allen pores over the Mexican guidebook that we bought for him in Vancouver. Dag looks through their Spanish grammar book, and puts together an impromptu quiz.

"OK, Allen, how do you say this in Spanish: Where is the nearest beach? I want to build a boat here. Can we rent this cabin for three months? Do you have a saw?"

Allen faultlessly translates every sentence. His memory is astonishing. Just before we go to bed he gives us a word-perfect recital of Robert Service's *The Cremation of Sam McGee*—all fourteen verses of it.

"In the old days, everyone could recite poetry," he tells us. "We used to sit around in the evenings just like this, entertaining each other. Then radio came along, and spoiled everything."

JULY 23 ■ We wake to an overcast sky, and a light breeze that wafts the smoke from the stovepipe of *China Cloud* over to us. The Farrells are going through their usual morning routine—once Allen's lit the fire, he plays his ukulele while Sharie makes breakfast. After they've eaten he takes her pulse and blood pressure, and through the porthole we hear the *peep peep peep!* as the machine makes its reading. At the beginning of our journey together, this intimacy made me uneasy; I worried about invading the Farrells' privacy, about bothering them with our constant closeness. Now, it feels strange if we're not rafted up together, able to easily step from our deck to theirs, to call to them through the portholes, to have the sense of being physically connected. The term "needing space" means little to Allen and Sharie. We've learned not to disturb them when Allen is painting or they're learning Spanish, and to tactfully withdraw so they can have their afternoon nap and get to bed early at night. But left on their own for too long, they grow lonesome and crave company.

"It's easier for people to love each other when they live closely," Sharie told me yesterday.

As they settle down for half an hour's Spanish practice, we listen to a weather report. Northwest winds are forecast at the northern end of the Strait of Georgia, and southeast winds at the south.

"Great," says Dag sardonically. "We're right in the middle."

A view across Malaspina Strait.

By half past nine we're ghosting out of Maude Bay. Behind us, Jervis Inlet is wreathed in a grey mist. The light breezes flowing out of it nudge us towards Scotch Fir Point. Just before we reach it, the wind dies, and for a couple of hours we drift. Around noon, a dark threatening cloud builds over Texada Island, and soon scraps of it are being torn off by a building southerly wind.

"There's no protected anchorage between here and Powell River," hollers Allen as *China Cloud* sails by. "I sure hope we don't lose this wind. Maybe we'll get to Van Anda and visit Terrible Ted."

Dag sets the sail on a broad reach and points the bow across Malaspina Strait towards Texada Island. Its eastern shoreline is scarred by mining and logging, and for thirty miles or so it rises steeply from the water, offering few safe harbours for boats. We're not the first to sense something foreboding about Texada—according to local lore, native peoples fled the island many years ago because they believed it was about to sink beneath the ocean.

The best bet for anchorage close to Van Anda is Sturt Bay, so we're puzzled to see *China Cloud,* a mile ahead of us, heading towards an unprotected cove open to the southeast winds.

"Allen's only been here a few times, years ago," says Dag worriedly. "And his eyesight is so poor these days, if he doesn't have familiar landmarks to guide him he can easily go the wrong way."

China Cloud's sails slip from sight behind land, then quickly reappear as Allen turns the boat and heads out again. In the meantime we've had the chance to catch up, and we're not far behind Allen by the time he drops anchor close to the public float in Van Anda Cove. We find him striding about the deck, obviously agitated.

"All that drifting around we did earlier was awful!" he cries as we raft up.

"This seems like a pretty exposed spot, Allen," says Dag, throwing our bow line to him. "The northwesterlies must come ripping in here."

"I know! What are we doing here?"

The bay is lined with houses, and from a garden a woman yells, "Are you lost?" Both Allen and Dag looked momentarily piqued.

"We're looking for Ted Soepboer," Allen calls back.

"Go around into Sturt Bay. I'll phone him."

By the time we've sailed around Marble Bluff, Ted and Barb Soepboer are waiting for us on the dock in Sturt Bay. He's a powerfully built man, with a neatly trimmed goatee and prematurely silver hair. His wife is slender, and looks shy. There's an old-fashioned air about the couple, and they seem wholesome and well-meaning.

"Allen and Sharie, it's so good to see you!" cries Ted. "When my neighbour rang I said, 'Wife, let's get going, we've got to watch *China Cloud* sail in.' What a sight! It's the most beautiful boat on the whole coast!"

He points behind him to a wooden scow tied up at the float. It's squat and robust, like Ted. He and Barb were sailing it when they first met Allen and Sharie, aboard *China Cloud,* in Montague Harbour.

"You remember my old scow, Allen? It's for sale if you know anyone who wants it. It's comfortable to travel in, but we need something bigger, so we can live aboard all the time."

Ted Soepboer was born on a canal boat in Holland, and he claims water is in his blood. He's lived on Texada Island for the last seven years, and now he's itching to be afloat again.

"I've had enough of the land and this house business. I want to hoist the anchor and go. You'd like that too, wouldn't you, Barb?"

Before Barb can confirm or deny this, Ted carries on.

"My Barb doesn't look so strong, but she is. One time we were in the bush, trying to find a new mast. I figured out the right tree, but to bring it down I needed a rope tied to the top, so I said, 'Wife, climb up there.' I weighed two hundred and fifty pounds and I figured if I fell and got hurt, she'd never be able to pack me out of the bush. Whereas if *she* fell I could easily get her out, and anyway I'd probably catch her on the way down, eh?"

"I wasn't keen on climbing that tree," says Barb quietly. "But I did it."

They invite us to come to their house for dinner tomorrow, and Ted reminds Allen that he wants his advice on the boat he's building.

"I'm making it mostly out of beachcombed wood, and it won't have a smelly engine. We used to have a steel boat, and I said to Barb, 'Don't ever hit anything in this, because if it's one of those plastic tubs we'll cut right through it and never even notice.' Well, it was a mistake telling her that. The first harbour we came into, she started jumping round and squawking when we got anywhere near another boat. It was like having a hysterical seagull on board. I said, 'Wife, get below out of sight, and make me a cup of coffee quick.' Know why, Allen? One time, an American told me, 'Whenever you manoeuvre through a harbour, always have a cup of coffee in one hand. Then it doesn't matter how white your knuckles are, from a distance you'll look relaxed!' "

After setting a time to visit Ted and Barb, we return to our boats, which are anchored close to the limestone excavations on the far shore. There has been mining on Texada Island since 1876, when a whaler named Trim found some iron ore deposits. Copper, gold, silver and marble were quickly discovered, and a boom was on. People flocked to Van Anda, and by 1910 the little settlement had grown to encompass three thousand inhabitants, three hotels and saloons, a hospital, a school, several stores, a jail, its own newspaper and the only opera house north of San Francisco. A series of fires destroyed most of the buildings, and soon after the First World War the iron market collapsed. These days only about four hundred people live in Van Anda, and the population of the entire island barely scrapes one and a half thousand.

J U L Y 2 4 ■ In Ted and Barb's garden is a shed containing the frame of another squat, hefty boat. Ted shows Allen around it, slapping its large, closely spaced floor timbers and ribs.

"She's thirty-two feet, and a bit like a dory. And she's all my own design. People ask me about blueprints, Allen, and I tell them, 'What do you think I'm building, a watch?' I got the blueprints in my head. That way, they can't get dirty and they can't blow away."

As Allen clambers around the boat, examining her in detail, Ted bombards him with questions.

"Can I bend these planks along the hull without steaming them? Should I butt them up to each other or use scarf joints? What's the best way to mount the gudgeon? Is she strong enough, Allen? She's got six-by-six floor timbers, and three-by-six ribs. I don't want to under-build her."

"I don't think there's any danger of that Ted," says Allen wondering-ly. "But, oh boy, she'll be pretty heavy. Do you think she'll go to windward?"

Barb has prepared a huge roast pork dinner, with all the trimmings. She heaps our plates with slabs of meat, homegrown vegetables, piping hot gravy. After two helpings of everything, Ted says, "Wife, these people are still hungry. What's for dessert?"

In unison we all beg for a break so we can rest our stomachs. I help Barb clear away the dishes, while Ted talks to Allen and Sharie, leaning towards them with his forearms resting on the table.

"Look at those arms!" cries Sharie. "They're enormous!"

"They give me problems," he tells her, in all seriousness. "I can't reach round with them to wash my back. We won't have an engine on the boat, but I'll have a shower. A bath's no good for me."

At last I pluck up the courage to ask him why he's known as Terrible Ted.

"Oh, that's an old name, there was a reason for it. I've calmed down so much now that I get nervous when my wife shouts at me."

Ted Soepboer shows Allen the model of his new boat.

"Tell them, Ted," says Barb fondly, sitting next to him and wiping her hands on a tea towel.

With a little more prompting, the story unfolds. Ted used to live in Kaslo, where he worked as a strong man. He performed at logger shows, bending crowbars, doing press-ups with a three-hundred-pound man on his back, pulling trucks with a rope over his shoulder. Before that he was a wrestler, and took on the role of the "bad guy." Terrible Ted was his wrestling name, but it stuck.

"Everyone in Kaslo knew me. When kids saw me, they'd scream, 'It's Terrible Ted, it's Terrible Ted!' So I'd roar and run after them, playing the game, eh?"

From time to time he worked for prospectors, packing their gear into the bush. A few of his clients were geologists, newly graduated from school.

"Some of these guys couldn't sharpen an axe without cutting their foot, or light a fire without burning their face. And if they saw a bear they'd be so scared they'd want me to shoot it. But I didn't want to do that! I love animals."

Ted used to have a pet bear. It started coming around his house when it was young; Ted fed it and soon it was tame. Then it took to following him into town. One day the RCMP called round and said people in Kaslo were getting concerned about Terrible Ted's bear, that if it came into town again they'd have to shoot it. So he tied it up whenever he went out.

"One day, I was in town and someone said, 'Ted, your bear's over there by the garbage.' I went up to him, he had garbage all over his nose, and he seemed pretty annoyed to see me. I said, 'Sorry, but I have to do this for your own good,' and I took off my belt and put it around his neck. That bear, he put up a bit of a struggle on the way home—he dragged me along the ground, halfway across the golf course. And then, when I got back, there on the porch was—"

"Your bear!" we chorus.

"Yep. Lying with his head on his paws, waiting for me."

It's an apocryphal story, told in various forms along the coast. But, in Ted's case, I'm certain that it's true.

JULY 25 ■ Out in Malaspina Strait, the wind blows southeast at thirty knots. Swells roll into the bay, and we drag anchor with *China Cloud,* almost ending up on top of a log boom. Allen and Dag row to the beach in the dory, and secure a shore line. After a few hours of sitting hunched under our canopy, hiding from the rain, I grow restless and decide to go and explore Van Anda.

At the top of the jetty in Sturt Bay stands Texada Island's equivalent of a billboard: a log, six feet in diameter and twelve feet long, engraved with the words, "ACE'S BAR AND GRILL." Opposite it, across a dirt track, a cliff face has been dynamited to form a parking lot. Boulders and gravel are strewn over it, and nailed to a power pole there's a large sign saying "NO CAMPING." The dirt track turns into a blacktopped road, which leads me through a residential area, by a school ballpark, and past some buildings with blackberry bushes and fireweed growing beside them. There's a supermarket, a post office, a bank, a gas station and an office supply shop which also serves as a coffee bar and bakery. Suddenly I realize that this is Van Anda. There's hardly a soul about, and only the occasional pickup truck driving by. I feel oddly out of place.

The cashier in the supermarket looks at me a little suspiciously when I buy cheese and grapes. In the coffee bar, a couple of men watch me curiously as I scribble a letter, but avert their eyes when I turn to them to strike up a conversation. The post office clerk is friendly—so much so that she manages to glean a good deal of my life history while selling me a book of stamps.

Back on *China Cloud,* Allen is on deck, emptying the bilge with his built-in pump. It's a simple, but effective system—a square column of cedar boards with a leather flap in the bottom, and a long wooden plunger with copper spikes and a leather flap on the end. As he pumps, water spills over the top of the column, across the deck and through the scuppers.

"This pump doesn't need electricity, it doesn't rust and it's nice and quiet," he tells me. "And you can build it any size you like. Everybody had them in the old days."

While I was in Van Anda Allen tried to paint, but was frustrated by the poor light.

"This weather is awful," I commiserate.

"I don't mind the southeast winds when I'm sailing," he says. "They build up gradually, over two or three hours, so you've got time to decide what to do. But with the west or northwest, you've only got minutes. You see it coming and then the sharp edge of the front hits you, full force."

All night, the wind howls out in the channel, and rain lashes against our canopy. I dream that Dag and I are out in the middle of the Atlantic aboard *Luna Moth* when a huge wave crashes over us, sweeping away our mast, rigging and oar, and leaving us helplessly adrift in a vast, indifferent ocean.

J U L Y   2 6   ■   By half past eight we're out in the strait. According to the weather radio, the wind is blowing twenty-six knots and gusting at Grief Point, just a few miles to the south. Both sea and sky are a dark, angry grey, and low clouds race over our heads. I've got everything safely stowed away, and the emergency box with the radio at hand. As the wind builds, Dag twice tells me to reef down. I sit next to him, leaning out over the water as far as I dare to counter the heeling of the boat,

The "sharp edge" of a front moves towards Luna Moth, *south of the Copeland Islands.*

hanging on with a white-knuckled grip and wishing desperately I was somewhere warm, dry and steady underfoot.

After an hour, the wind calms enough for us to shake out the reefs. We scoot northwards towards the mainland, watching the pillars of smoke issuing from the Powell River pulp mill grow steadily bigger.

"The wind is forecast to switch to northwest early this afternoon," says Dag, who is thoroughly enjoying himself. "At this rate we might reach Sarah Point just in time to catch the switch and get blown up Desolation Sound."

I've just begun to relax when a gust of wind scours across the water and bangs into our sail. A second later there's a horribly familiar *CRACK!* Automatically, I reach for the halyard and uncleat it. When nothing happens I scuttle like a crab along the listing deck towards the mast. Halfway there, I freeze. The mast has jumped out of its step and is leaning over, only held in place by the thwart.

"Pull down the sail!" yells Dag. "No, forget it, get back here and take the tiller!"

He rushes to the prow, balances precariously on the gunwale of the tossing boat, and starts grappling with the thirty-foot mast.

"Keep her nose into the wind!"

It's hard to concentrate on steering, for Dag looks about to tumble backwards into the waves at any moment. Frantically, and in vain, I try to remember how to execute the "man-overboard manoeuvre." Minutes tick by, as we wallow in the building waves and Dag continues to struggle. Finally he heaves, lurches forward with the mast and drops it into its step.

"Man, that was close," he says, taking over the tiller. "It should be okay now, as long as we take it easy."

China Cloud has hove to in the lee of Grief Point, where the wind and water are a little quieter. With only two panels up, we hobble towards her. When we're almost alongside, Allen sets off again northwards, towards Harwood Island. We yell to him that we're having problems with our mast, but the wind carelessly whips away our words. A broad shaft of sunlight breaks through the clouds, and from behind the island a double rainbow arches heavenward. My hope that this is an auspicious sign soon fades. Two big power boats appear in the distance, heading south at speed, right on course for us. One passes to our starboard, the other to our port. As their wakes meet the waves, a chaotic chop develops. This time we're braced for the worst, and as the mast comes out of its step and leans we're already spinning into a routine—Dag rushing forward while I drop the sail and then man the tiller.

"At least the wind is nice and steady now," he calls, when finally the mast is in place again. "We'll just have to try and avoid those wakes. Hang onto the tiller, I'm going to make some wedges to put around the base of the mast."

As he crouches down, chopping and hammering, Allen turns *China Cloud* and comes alongside to find out why we're so slow. Dag shouts an explanation, and insists that we'll be all right.

"Let's try for the Ragged Islands," Allen suggests, "and anchor in there if necessary. I'll keep close to you."

What Allen calls the Ragged Islands are now known as the Copelands, renamed in 1945 after Joe Copeland, a Confederate soldier and stagecoach robber who settled around here at the end of last century. Between the Copelands and the mainland is Thulin Passage, a thoroughfare for boats travelling to and from Desolation Sound. We're just north of Savary Island when several motorboats emerge from this passage. As the little flotilla approaches, Dag looks behind, and curses under his breath. An enormous launch is bearing down on us from the south. I wave frantically, signalling its skipper to steer away. People aboard wave back, and start videoing. The launch passes close to *China Cloud*'s starboard side, just as three motorboats zip by us to port.

"Bloody stink pots!" Allen yells in fury. Turning in our direction, he hollers, "Take the waves on the beam!"

This time, when the mast pops out, Dag is already standing on the prow, ready to resume his Sisyphean task. Once back at the tiller, he starts following Allen, who is steering towards the outside of the south-ernmost Copeland Islands.

"I thought we were anchoring in the Copelands, Dag?"

"It's best to keep away from the motorboats coming out of Thulin Passage," he explains. "And Allen probably thinks we can make it up to Sarah Point before the wind switches."

"Isn't that a bit of a gamble?" I ask weakly.

He doesn't reply; he's scrutinizing the sky to the northwest. A massive cloud with a deep dark belly is barrelling towards us. Below it, on the horizon, is a strip of clear sky, the sign of a big wind moving in.

"Here comes Allen's 'sharp edge' of the front," says Dag tersely, and changes course for Thulin Passage.

Minutes later, the squall hits. Rain lashes our faces and the wind kicks up a short, steep chop. Again the mast pops out of its step, and this time Dag has a terrible struggle, fighting to keep his balance as the boat is tossed about. Meanwhile we are drifting towards the lee shore; when the mast is back in place, Dag quickly drops the anchor, praying this will stop us being battered against the rocks that are looming ever closer. According to our chart there's a steep dropoff, so he lets out all the line.

"God, I hope it'll take hold," he yells, over the din of wind and flapping cloth.

The line goes taut. We relax slightly, but it's obvious we can't sit for long in such an exposed place.

"Let's radio for help," I urge Dag, "and get someone to tow us to safety."

"I'm not accepting a tow," he retorts. "When the wind dies down I'll yuloh to Lund. You'll have to go forward and hang onto the mast."

"What if it goes again? We could lose it next time!"

We're still arguing when Allen arrives and settles the matter. I hear the rush of *China Cloud*'s bow wave as she sails up to our port side. Allen calls that he will tow us, and after we hoist the anchor, he steers in close to *Luna Moth* and throws us a line. Once we're tied on, he drops his mainsail. Slowly, slowly, we head south towards Lund, me at the tiller, Dag clutching the mast.

In the shelter of Sevilla Island, Dag lets go the tow line and yulohs along behind *China Cloud* into Finn Bay. In the forties and fifties, Allen and Sharie often anchored here. But as a fishing boat chugs by, a man leans out from the wheelhouse to tell us that we can't put our hooks down because sewer pipes have been laid across the bay. Disgruntled by this, Allen ties up to an old floating barge instead of the government dock, and we raft up alongside. Finn Bay is a picturesque little place. Named after the nationality of its first white settlers, it is a quiet backwater compared to the bustling scene at Lund, half a mile to the south. Old boat houses and net lofts built of weathered grey boards are still in use, and boardwalks cross the rocks that connect Sevilla Island to the mainland. Lying on the beach above the high tide mark are some big, red wooden boxes.

"They're old cod boxes," Allen explains. "You put them in the water and kept live cod in them. They belonged to Walt. He was a fisherman here. He's probably gone now. Or maybe he's an old man, sitting and looking at us through his window."

Straightaway, he and Dag set to work on hoisting our mast. When it's up, we all gaze in dismay at the base. It looks like a well-chewed lollipop stick—a mass of pulped, mushy fibres.

"I was worried from the start about it being too loose in its step," admits Dag. "It was always banging around a bit."

"I'm surprised it lasted so long," says Allen. "Want to borrow my saw again? You're becoming an expert at this."

To make up for scuttling the Farrells' hopes of reaching Desolation Sound today, we invite them out for dinner in Lund.

"Thank goodness we're not anchored here," says Allen, as he steers the dory towards the crowded dock, through scores of boats. During the winter Lund is a quiet community of about five hundred people. Right now it's bustling with tourists, a sight that would have gladdened the hearts of its founders, Charles and Fred Thulin. In 1889 these enterprising siblings named the settlement after a university town in their native Sweden. During the next few years they developed the sheltered harbour as a place steam tugs could call into for water and cordwood. They opened a hotel, store and post office, obtained the first liquor licence north of Vancouver, built their own steamboat and brought in one of the first up-coast donkey engines for logging. By 1905 they had expanded their store and built a bigger hotel, which still stands today. And, to Allen and Sharie's delight, the specialty of the day in its café is roast pork, served with mashed potatoes and gravy.

"*Real* food!" says Allen. "Like in the old days!"

CHAPTER NINE

Desolation Sound

JULY 27 ■ "Allen says he just had the best sleep for ages," Sharie calls down to us, "because of all the meat he ate last night!"

The day has started out coolish and cloudy, with a light northwest wind. There's a general consensus that we should move, but no one is in much of a hurry. The morning slips by. Allen paints, Sharie catches up on correspondence, I make notes and Dag goes off in the kayak to do some photography. By noon the sky is clearing and just as we finish lunch a west wind picks up. The Farrells decide to forfeit their post-prandial nap, and by two o'clock we're headed out of Lund, sailing close-hauled to windward, attempting to clear the southernmost of the Copeland Islands in one tack.

"Look, Maria," says Dag jubilantly. "We're actually beating *China Cloud!*" It's the first and probably the last time. The conditions are perfect —just the right amount of wind for us, not quite enough for Allen. His competitive streak emerges—he keeps fiddling with his sails, but still he's forced to tack. It's a short-lived triumph, however; when we change course to northwards, along the outside of the Copelands, *China Cloud* soon passes *Luna Moth,* with Allen beaming at us from the cockpit.

The honeycombed rocks along the shores of the Copelands are splashed with colour—greys and orange of lichen above the high tide mark, browns and russet of seaweed below. Hernando and Twin islands lie to the north, Major Island is to our port, and behind us are the gleaming sand beaches of Savary Island. Gulls wheel and soar above us, crying out as if in appreciation of the glorious afternoon, the sparkling water, the clouds shaped like castles and fish and monsters hanging in a cerulean sky.

We slip by Bliss Landing, and the snow cone of Mount Denman. Ahead lies Sarah Point. Once around it, we'll see up into Homfray Channel. The vista awaiting us has been so heaped with praise by other sailors that I'm prepared for disappointment, but, as we skirt the headland, I find myself stupefied by its scale, its grandeur, its splendour. Mile-high mountains drop straight from snowy peaks to the ocean. In the sounds between them, sheer islands rise up, darkly clad in dense green forest. The wind is behind us now and *China Cloud* pulls away, dwarfed by the giants around her and the expanses of water ahead, until she seems a mere speck in this immense landscape. Finally she disappears behind Marylebone Point on West Redonda Island. Half an hour later we round the point. Ahead we see only the empty stretch of Waddington Channel, branching off towards Pendrell Sound.

"Surely *China Cloud* can't have made it into Pendrell already?" muses Dag.

Then we spy her, at anchor inside the mouth of Roscoe Bay, bathed in early evening sunlight.

"The scenery was so beautiful coming up here today," says Sharie, as we raft up. "It took me right back to the old days."

JULY 28 ■ Pushed by the slightest of breezes, and still rafted to *China Cloud,* in ten minutes we ghost to the head of narrow, steep-sided Roscoe Bay.

"That's exactly the right amount of sailing for one day," says Allen, as he drops the anchor.

On the shore of West Redonda Island, an old flume runs alongside the creek that flows from Black Lake into the bay.

"I remember playing in a log flume somewhere around here when I was seven years old," Allen tells us. "I had no idea how dangerous it was—some logs ran half a mile down the mountain, picking up speed and bouncing along."

For several years Allen's father travelled along the coast, working as a surveyor and mapper for the Forestry Department.

"We stayed with him at different camps—Blind Bay, Thurston Bay. He'd go off into the bush with measuring chains and a compass. Sometimes I'd go with him and set the compass. I'd line up one tree with the northwest, follow it, then line up the next. I developed a good eye that way."

In the late forties Allen returned here with Sharie and Keray, aboard *Wind Song*.

"One time in Toba Inlet, we found an old steam donkey used for logging, high up on the mountainside. We decided its fire grid would be good ballast for *Wind Song*. Keray and I got it down the hill somehow, rolling and pushing it along, then we cemented it into place alongside the keel."

They came across many deserted settlements in the sound, and collected fruit from old orchards. Close to here, by Black Lake, they found Gravenstein apples.

"An Indian friend of ours told us how to dry the fruit on cedar racks over the wood stove," Allen recalls. "He said the wood smoke killed the worms. I don't know if that was true. But we had several tiers of racks, and some of the fruit lasted four years."

JULY 29 ■ This is the noisiest, most crowded anchorage we've been to all summer. Loud music drifts from boats, generators run for hours on end, and people constantly buzz by in motorized tenders. Allen is dismayed by the temperature of the water, which around here can reach up to seventy-five degrees at this time of year.

"Only sixty-seven degrees!" he cries, pulling the thermometer out of the water for the third time this morning. "What's going on?"

A Zodiac with a couple in it goes by, close to *China Cloud*.

"Hey Phyllis, look at that funky boat," shouts the man to his wife, unaware that we can hear him over the engine. "I wonder how that old guy manages to sail it?"

A fibreglass dingy zips up next. It's driven by a teenage boy dressed in long baggy shorts, and with his hair in dreadlocks. He lets the engine idle while he admires *China Cloud*.

"That's an awesome boat, man!" he yells to Allen. "It's rad!"

"Oh, thank you," says Allen politely.

As the boy zooms off, he turns to me with a perplexed expression. "What did he mean?"

J U L Y 3 0 ■ Mount Addenbrook, on East Redonda Island, is shrouded in swirling mist, and clouds hang low over Roscoe Bay. In the main cabin of *China Cloud* the stove is crackling, we're all drinking cocoa, and I'm reading out a true story about a shipwreck off the east coast of the States, written by one of the survivors. It's a gruesome account of being adrift for days in a life raft without food or water. One person dies of septicemia, and two more drink seawater, go insane and throw themselves to the sharks.

"Wow," says Allen when I've finished. "Who would be stupid enough to go sailing offshore?"

There's a knock on the hull, and two faces familiar to us all appear at a porthole. Danny and Gailee Norrie work the winters in Los Angeles and spend every summer in the Strait of Georgia aboard their thirty-five-foot cutter, *Dark Star*. They first met Allen and Sharie ten years ago at a picnic on Newcastle Island, across from Nanaimo.

"This guy with long white hair was climbing trees, walking on his hands and doing somersaults," recalls Danny. "I got talking to him, and he mentioned being worried about one of his sons. He said, 'Now that Barrie has turned fifty, I hope he'll start taking my advice.' My jaw dropped—I couldn't believe I was looking at a guy old enough to have a fifty-year-old son!"

After lunch the sun comes out, and we go to swim and wash in Black Lake. Allen has a sack with him, and on the way we collect pine needles for Mario's litter box. Sharie admires the ladyslipper growing along the path; Allen gazes at young cedars and says, "Look at all those battens for sails!"

Lying on some flat rocks are several groups of people from other boats anchored in Roscoe Bay. As we peel off our clothes they glance curiously at Gailee, with hair flowing to her hips like a wood nymph, and at Allen, who is in better shape than most men half his age.

J U L Y   3 1   ■   At dawn, Roscoe Bay is quiet save for the rushing of a waterfall down the steep valley wall, and the high-pitched whistles of red-beaked oyster catchers picking their way over the rocks on shore. I sit on deck, sadly considering the fact that our trip is almost over. Soon, we will head south again: the Farrells will say their goodbyes, dispose of their belongings and give away their boat, and Dag and I will return to our other existence, ashore. Reaching over, I run my hand along the black hull of *China Cloud*. We've spent so many days and nights rafted up like this, living closely together with Allen and Sharie. Our daily lives have become entwined with theirs, our rhythms are now in sync. It's hard to imagine that in a few days we'll be apart. From inside the boat I hear a mewing, then Mario sticks his head through an open porthole.

"Where to next, puss?" I whisper, scratching him behind the ears. He regards me solemnly, as if he's been wondering that himself.

After breakfast we decided to leave Roscoe Bay, and I join the Farrells on *China Cloud* for the day's sail. Allen sculls out and Dag is doing the same right behind; our boats look like a mother and her baby. The water in Waddington Channel is so flat calm that Mario, who usually hides under the cabin table while the boat is under sail, comes up on deck. He sprawls in front of the cockpit, lying on his back and inviting us to rub his belly.

"That's a bad sign," says Allen. "I bet there'll be no wind today. Where do you think we'll get to?"

Light, shifting breezes blow up during the morning. We wander about, first in the direction of Prideaux Haven, then towards the gap between Mink Island and the mainland. Dag sails along behind us, keeping pace. *Dark Star* falls back, and from time to time we hear a rumbling as Danny starts up the engine. On *China Cloud* we're all relaxed, enjoying the sun, the splendid scenery and each other's company. Allen and Sharie reminisce about the winter they spent up here in the late forties, when they dug thirteen tons of clams and made two hundred dollars for their trip to Fiji.

"In those days you got three and a half cents a pound for manila clams, and four cents a pound for littlenecks," says Allen, "and there were

Allen, Sharie and Keray aboard Wind Song, *circa 1951.*

no restrictions. First we dug in Malaspina Inlet, but we only managed to get half a bucket of clams. Then we went to Theodosia Inlet and dug for seven nights, during the lowest tides of the month. It was terrible work. In winter the low tides are at night, so we'd be out in the dark and the cold. We had to shake our hands to keep them warm. We washed the clams in a slatted wooden box on deck, and kept them in buckets of saltwater to stop them freezing. Once Sharie cried and said, 'There must be an easier way to make a living!' "

To their dismay, when they tried to sell their harvest they found that no one was buying any clams. Just as they were about to run out of food and money, they arrived at Bliss Landing, where the store owner, Loyal Young, bought their clams on spec for seven dollars.

"I think he took them just out of kindness," says Sharie. "Anyway, he and his wife, Betty, became good friends. They were always inviting us up for dinner. The boat would come in with supplies for his shop, and he'd call us over and insist on feeding us with the food that should have been for sale in his store."

We're moving, very slowly, past Bold Point. Behind it is Tenedos Bay, where Allen and Sharie hit their clam jackpot—three thousand pounds of clams during a seven-day tide. Brimming with excitement, they hurried with them to Bliss Landing, where they discovered the buyers were only accepting littleneck clams.

"Of course, our clams were all mixed up," Allen recalls. "So Loyal set up these wire racks on the beach by his fish scow, and he brought out a radio, and his kids came and the whole family worked with us for three days and nights, sorting the manilas from the littlenecks. In the end we had one and a half thousand pounds of littlenecks to sell. We put the manilas back on the beach."

We have lunch on deck: plates of chapattis, cheese and butter that Sharie passes to the cockpit through the cabin's sliding window. When it's time for the Farrells to take their nap, I offer to steer *China Cloud*.

"Where to?" I ask Allen.

"That's up to you," he answers. "You're the skipper now."

By three o'clock, when Allen and Sharie wake, we're approaching the Gifford Peninsula. A group of kayakers paddles by, easily overtaking *China Cloud* and *Luna Moth*. In six hours we've barely covered six miles. I'm enjoying drifting, and for once Allen and Sharie don't seem to mind it either. Allen brings out his ukulele, and we sing "Who's Sorry Now?" "Goodnight Irene" and "Hang Down Your Head Tom Dooley." I've never played an instrument in my life, but within half an hour Allen has managed to teach me the three chords of "Tom Dooley," and I strum while he and Sharie sing. It's blissful to be sailing on this magical boat through some of the most magnificent scenery in the world, crooning and sharing stories with two people I love. But lurking behind the joy is a trace of sorrow. As each day goes by, the realization sinks in that this is the Farrells' last cruise on *China Cloud,* that they won't be coming this way again aboard her—or, perhaps, on any other boat.

I sit in silence for a while. Sensing something is wrong, Sharie lays a hand on my arm.

"Shall we have some tea?" she asks.

While the kettle boils I search the cabin for the cookie jar, which Sharie has been unable to find all day. I've given up looking and am on my way back to the cockpit, when a glint of something catches my eye.

"It's in the dory!" I cry.

"I remember now," says Sharie. "I took it with me last night when we went over to *Dark Star* for dinner."

"It's easy to lose things on a boat," says Allen. "I lost a pair of binoculars off the deck not long ago."

"When?" I ask. "On this trip?"

"Oh, no, sometime around 1958."

By the time we've finished our tea, the wind has died completely. Allen yulohs for half an hour, and then I try. It takes a few minutes to get the motion—rocking back and forth on the balls of my feet, using my body weight to sweep the long oar in a figure-of-eight motion. Gazing at the water, I see bubbles going by. Miraculously, I'm managing to move this forty-foot, six-ton boat with only my own strength.

"She's shaped like an Indian canoe, so maybe that's why you can scull her so well," says Allen. "And she's built mostly from cedar, which is half the weight of other woods, so she's light."

Light, just like the Farrells, I think; they have so few possessions, such little needs, everything about their lifestyle is light and flexible.

I scull for almost an hour, enjoying the rhythm, and the sense of propelling the boat with my body. When a puff of wind comes up, I rest. The sheer walls of West Redonda Island, across Homfray Channel, are in shadow by the time we sail into Galley Bay. Sharie is intensely quiet as we skirt around the sprinkling of small uninhabited islands in its mouth, towards a protected anchorage. She first saw this place fifty-six years ago with George Dibbern and Eileen Morris, from the deck of

Allen croons while manning the tiller in Desolation Sound.

Te Rapunga. After weeks of searching the coast for a place where they could live in harmony with nature, they arrived here and realized they'd found it.

"We were so enchanted that we could not tear ourselves away from the place," Dibbern wrote in *Ship Without A Port,* "but lived there in a dream. . . . In our minds we made tracks through the woods. . . . planted fruit trees, built a long low log cabin . . . built other little cabins here and there. . . ."

Next to me, Sharie sighs. "When Eileen and I bought land here we forgot to register for ownership of these islands. George was really mad about that."

"I don't blame him," I tease her.

"Isn't it a lovely place?" She gazes around the generously curving bay, and at the handful of houses peeking out from among the trees on shore. "I feel envious of the people who live here now. Maybe I shouldn't have sold the land."

"What's the point of regretting it?" Allen snaps. "Who wants to have land and a house to worry about?"

It wasn't until the fifties that Eileen and Sharie sold their two hundred acres. When the Farrells went to Fiji in 1951, they'd stored their belongings here in a small shed. While they were away, someone looted the shed and stole everything.

"They were welcome to it," says Allen. He turns to me. "Don't collect stuff—remember that."

Seals pop their heads above the water and regard us curiously. A heron stands meditatively in the shallows. Out in the channel, Station Island is a friendly dark green hump, and behind it other islands and mountains stretch away in blue, violet and purple layers.

"So why didn't you just come and live here in 1952 instead of buying land in Blind Bay?" I ask.

Allen and Sharie look at each other.

"I don't know," she says.

"Why didn't we?" Allen asks her. "Maybe we forgot about it!"

We drop anchor at seven o'clock, ten hours and approximately ten miles after we set out. Before long, a crescent moon climbs into a clear, pale blue sky. We settle down for the night, lulled to sleep by the hooting of an owl.

A U G 1   ■   "Let's go to Sharie's old property and find her lake," Allen suggests. George Dibbern had hoped to pipe water and generate electricity for their community from this trout lake. Later, Allen named it after Sharie, because she liked to go swimming there.

On the beach, while Allen secures the dory by tying a rope around a boulder, Sharie and I examine a campsite. A tarp spread over a frame of branches covers a driftwood table and bench, and shelves filled with pots, plates and jars.

"That looks like a nice place," she says appraisingly.

Over the last few days, Allen has been talking more about the possibility of them returning to Nelson Island next summer, and camping out while he builds a float house.

"Can you really imagine living somewhere like this, Sharie?" I ask her. She leans on her staff, and considers.

"I've always loved camping. Allen and I have done it a lot. We camped on beaches when we came up the coast looking for land, and when we rowed around Lasqueti. And we lived under a tarp for months when we were helping Keray build his big log house in Westview. As long as it's warm and dry and I have somewhere comfortable to sleep, I'll be happy."

The path to the lake goes by a house. Roses bloom around it, and nasturtiums spill out of cedar boxes. A man sits on the deck, watching our approach. His eyes wander over the towels and wash bags we're carrying.

"The lake is on private land now," he tells us. "You're welcome to walk through the woods to it, but please don't swim or wash, as it provides our drinking water."

Sensing Allen bristle next to me, I quickly make introductions and explain how Sharie once owned this land. The man's face lights up; he's heard about the Farrells, and invites us onto his porch for a drink.

Carl Fairclough originally hails from North Manchester, in England. He works at the mill in Powell River, and this place is his summer home, built on one of the small lots Sharie's land was divided up into some years ago. Carl asks Sharie what originally brought her here. She's pensive for a few moments, as if gathering her thoughts, drawing them to her over almost six decades. When she speaks, her voice is soft and a little sad.

"Did you ever hear about George Dibbern? He was a German who sailed down to New Zealand and up to Canada in his thirty-foot boat—"

"Thirty-two feet, honey," Allen interrupts.

I fight back an urge to nudge him in the ribs, but Sharie only smiles fondly in his direction before continuing. She tells Carl the story of George arriving from New Zealand, and of sailing here with her and Eileen.

"There was a man in Galley Bay who couldn't keep up on his tax payments. He sold Eileen and me two hundred acres for $548. We had all sorts of plans, but then the war broke out and George and Eileen had to leave Canada. We sold the land in the fifties, to loggers. We got five thousand dollars for it, and Allen and I used our share to build *Ocean Girl*."

I walk behind the Farrells along the path to the lake. Sharie is elegant in a straw panama, a red wraparound skirt and a cream blouse. Again, time slips away, and I'm looking at a young, strong woman on

Allen and Sharie, circa 1975.

her way for a swim. But the forest around her belies the illusion. Its trees are spindly and evenly spaced, and fireweed is in flower between them.

"This was a lovely, old-growth forest," says Sharie. "Loyal Young at Bliss Landing was cross about us selling the land to loggers, he said it should have gone to someone who would have cared for it. But we didn't realize then how bad things could get."

The lake, too, has changed. Snags emerge from the dank, gloomy water, and we sink to our ankles in the muddy bottom. It's not a place for lingering, and we hurry away.

After supper on *China Cloud,* Allen pulls out a painting we've never seen before. Its colours are vivid and strong, and it depicts a small, shake-covered cabin on an islet.

"This is a different style for you, Allen!" exclaims Dag.

"That's because I didn't paint it," he says. "Sharie did."

She smiles shyly at our praise for her one and only painting, and confides that it's the cabin she'd always fantasized about building, here in the artists' community, before the war took that dream away.

A U G 2   ■ Sharie seems disturbed by memories. She's melan-
cholic, her blood pressure is higher than usual and she feels unwell. After
breakfast, while Allen practises Spanish, she lies down on her bunk. The
cat stretches out next to her and she reaches her long, fine fingers to
scratch his head.

"I'm really going to miss this bunk, and Mario," she says.

From out in Homfray Channel comes the long, loud blast of a horn.
Sharie lifts her head, her eyes wide in surprise.

"The Union Steamship's coming, honey!"

Then she laughs at herself, and lets her head fall back against the pillow.

A U G 3   ■ High summer is with us, and I want to stretch out
every minute of these halcyon days. I swim and swim, luxuriating in the
warm water, the sun, the scents of August. But Allen is restless. Now that
our journey is drawing to a close, he's impatient for the next stage. He's
anxious to give away *China Cloud,* and to get down to Mexico as soon
as he can.

"He's always been hasty," Sharie tells me, with her usual equanimi-
ty. "Once he's made up his mind about something, he can't wait to get
on with it."

For the last two nights he has slept badly, disturbed by a recurring
nightmare.

"I was in *China Cloud,* heading down some rapids at the bottom of
a deep canyon, completely out of control. I've had that dream about
every boat I've built."

"Sounds like an anxiety dream," I say. "You should take things
easy, Allen."

He can't relax. He works all day, learning Spanish, painting and
drawing, chopping kindling, fitting a new skylight above the galley area.
By midafternoon, when the air temperature is in the nineties, and the
water is a balmy seventy-two degrees, he finally agrees to join me in the
water as I'm having my fifth swim of the day. But he dons swimming
goggles and takes a brush with him to scrub algae off the copper on the
rudder and the bottom of the boat.

"I've got to make the boat perfect before we hand her over to
Gerry," he says.

AUG 4 ■ By seven o'clock, it's already hot. Dag and I swim over to the nearest island and wander around it naked. The ground is springy, covered by moss and mats of juniper with ripening berries. A couple of ravens scrutinize us from the branches of Garry oaks, discussing our presence in fluting calls. Two pileated woodpeckers pause from hacking away at a snag to watch us walk by. An olive-green snake slithers across our path, and disappears into the undergrowth. We gaze between arbutus trees at the breathtaking views of ocean, islands and mountains. This rocky little island seems to hold the essence of the beauty we've seen all summer, all along the Strait of Georgia. Perhaps, I think, it's where Sharie dreamed of building her cabin. But I decide not to ask her, fearful of stirring up too many memories.

AUG 5 ■ Our supplies are almost out, and Allen decides we should head over to the store at Refuge Cove to stock up for the journey south. We set off first in *Luna Moth,* knowing that *China Cloud* will soon catch us up. By ten o'clock we're crossing the calm waters of Homfray Channel, and basking in hot sunshine. I stare up at the lofty mountains behind the dramatic walls of East Redonda Island. Snowfields gleam against the blue sky, seeming close enough for me to reach out and feel the cold crystals between my fingers.

An inflow wind picks up, and *China Cloud* appears from Galley Bay. As she cruises past us, I'm struck by the realization that this is the end of our journey, our last sail together before we turn back. At the tiller Allen is barebacked, his eyes shaded by a visor. His hair looks pure white, and his arms are strong and tanned. Sharie sits next to him on a silk cushion. She's wearing her pink straw hat, and her red skirt is pulled back over her knees to let the sun on her legs. She smiles and waves to us as they go by.

"You don't see yourself as I do," I remember Allen saying to her, all those weeks ago, at the start of our journey, "up on deck in your lovely skirts, so slender and graceful."

My eyes fill with this scene—Allen and Sharie close together in the cockpit of *China Cloud,* their sails against the mountains, sunlight on the blue water around them—and I try to imprint it on my memory, before it is gone forever.

Allen Farrell collection

Ocean Girl *under full sail.*

"See that line of pale blue water on the horizon?" Dag's voice breaks into my thoughts. "We'll be losing our wind soon."

A little while later, *Luna Moth* is becalmed. We both go overboard to swim. Beneath us, in a sound gouged out by monstrous glaciers, are two hundred fathoms of water. I put my head beneath the surface, open my eyes for a few seconds and look into the bottomless depths. The sight is incomprehensible, a firmament devoid of stars or suns, emptier than space itself. Flipping over onto my back, I stare upwards, reassured by the sight of wheeling gulls, of puffy clouds shaped like flying saucers.

"There's a boat catching a bit of wind half a mile away," calls Dag. "Let's get back on board in case some of it comes our way, otherwise we might have to swim further than we expected."

Just before two o'clock we sail around the point sheltering Refuge Cove. Motor launches whizz by us, seaplanes roar over our masts. At the government dock, scores of boats are tied up and people are hurrying up and down the ramp leading to a handful of stores. *China Cloud* leads us past this mayhem to the head of the bay, near the outlet to Refuge Lagoon. No other boats are anchored here, and along the shore old shake-clad houses stand on pilings. Allen walks forward, dropping his sails and then the anchor. He puts a fender over the side for us, and for the last time we raft up.

"The real wind is out in the strait," he says. "We usually just get light breezes in Desolation Sound."

"Like in the goddamn Gulf Islands?" I tease him.

"That's right!"

Though we've come here to provision, it's with reluctance that we row and kayak over to the store at Refuge Cove. Waste water pumped from the launderette and showers has formed a soapy scum along the beach. People sitting on the decks of their motor boats are drinking beer and partying hard.

"Booze!" says Allen loudly, as we walk past them. "Bloody booze!"

The store is crammed with shoppers. Allen is shocked by its prices, and scandalized by its liquor outlet. He's all for storming back to the dory, but we persuade him to sit for a few minutes and share some ice-cream bars. We're just finishing them when we're met by Beth Hill, an author who interviewed the Farrells for one of her books. Her boat, the *Eliza Jane,* is tied up close by. She invites us aboard and promptly suggests we all have a sherry. There's a moment of uncomfortable silence. Allen is taken aback—his aversion to alcohol is well known and he's rarely offered any.

"No thank you," he says finally. "We're teetotallers."

Although we've been dry for weeks in respect to the Farrells, right now a glass of sherry has a certain appeal. But Allen gives us a meaningful look, and adds, "*All* of us are teetotallers."

Dag and I make a farewell dinner for Allen and Sharie and the Norries, who followed us here in *Dark Star.* Salmon salad, potatoes with crisp bacon and lashings of butter, fruit salad with whipped cream—it's all delicious, but I'm having trouble swallowing. Danny has brought news of the latest weather report: variable winds, southeasterlies in the south of the strait, northwesterlies in the north. As we eat, we discuss what to do. Allen and Sharie want to return to Blind Bay to say goodbye to their family and leave Mario with Keray. Then they'll call into Lasqueti Island to visit friends, before returning to Nanaimo and preparing for Mexico.

"You don't have to hurry away," insists Sharie. "Come with us. We're so used to having you along, I can't imagine anything else."

I'm opening my mouth to accept her offer, when Dag speaks up.

"We should start for home in the morning," he says firmly.

Like Allen, when it's time to leave he'd rather get on with it, and not linger painfully over goodbyes.

AUG 6   ■ Sharie is still in bed, so I hurry down the companion-way and squeeze past the table to her bunk, where she's lying with Mario at her feet. She sits up, feels for her hearing aid and slips it into her ear.

"Dag and Maria are leaving, honey," Allen calls from behind me. "They want to say goodbye."

"Leaving? Already?" she says. "Oh, no."

A huge lump has formed in my throat. I hug her as hard as I dare, conscious of her bones, as light as a bird's, and her soft, velvety skin. Blinded by tears, I stumble back onto *Luna Moth,* with all the things I wanted to say—about how precious this trip has been, how much it has taught me, how grateful I am to the Farrells—left unsaid.

Allen stands on deck as we drift away, waving to us. Then he turns, goes down the companionway, and pulls the hatch shut. He's got things to do. All summer we've been sailing back in time with him and Sharie, through eight decades of memories and stories, places and people along the coast. Now, he's eager to start shedding the past and preparing for the future, and the next big adventure.

CHAPTER TEN

Farewell

SEPT 3 ■ At five o'clock, we look out and see them sailing into the gap between Newcastle and Protection islands. Excitedly, we jump into our kayaks and paddle over to greet them.

"Come aboard!" calls Allen.

Dag grabs hold of the rub rail, and is pulled along at a couple of knots by *China Cloud*. I follow suit, but the bow of my kayak swings out until I'm broadside and losing my balance. The kayak flips, and for a couple of seconds I'm hanging upside down in the water. When I break the surface, my straw hat and sunglasses are still in place, *China Cloud* is sailing away, and Allen and Sharie are gazing down at me in puzzlement and consternation.

Ten minutes later they are anchored in the gap and I'm dripping all over their deck, dazed and happy.

"I've so missed our cups of tea together, Maria," Sharie tells me.

"You know," says Allen, "before we set off we had no idea how this trip would be. We'd never travelled with anyone like that before so we were a bit wary. But it turned out so well. We had a wonderful time."

The boat is higher above the waterline than we've ever seen her, and the cabin is almost bare, and bereft of Mario. Lying on one bench are two small shoulder bags, the Farrells' luggage for Mexico. When we're sitting around the table, Allen pulls a letter from his pocket.

"It's from Gerry Fossum. He's arranged to keep the boat in Esquimalt. He says he'll have her ready for us next summer, filled with kindling for the stove."

I look at him questioningly.

"Well? Are you going to take her back?"

He shakes his head.

"You know how I am. I like to cut ties."

SEPT 28 ■ This is Allen and Sharie's last night on *China Cloud*. Their plane for Mexico doesn't leave for a week, but all summer Allen has insisted he wants to be off the boat by the end of September. Tomorrow Danny and Gailee will take them in *Dark Star* across the Strait of Georgia to Horseshoe Bay. From there they'll catch a bus to the house of Allen's sister Kay, in West Vancouver. Next week we'll pick them up and drive them to the airport. Their shoulder bags are packed and ready. For their money and documents Allen has made two long cotton pouches which hang from strings around their waists. He opens his trouser fly and pulls out his pouch to show us.

"Good god, Allen," I say, looking at it dangling between his legs. "You'll be arrested for doing that in the airport!"

We arrange to come in the morning to see them off.

"Be here before nine," Allen warns. "We're leaving then, come what may."

SEPT 29 ■ By half past eight, Gerry Fossum is aboard *China Cloud*, and *Dark Star* is rafted up, ready for take-off. Allen and Sharie are just finishing their breakfast of porridge and toast. They're both a bit giddy with excitement, and Allen keeps looking at his watch. Suddenly he jumps up, and puts on his straw hat.

"Come on, honey!"

"There's no hurry," says Gailee.

"No, nine o'clock we're off," insists Allen. "Ready, honey?"

"I have to do the dishes first," Sharie tells him.

I wash up for her while she and Allen check they've got everything. Then suddenly we're all up on deck, looking at each other, stunned.

China Cloud *lies peacefully at anchor.*

"I forgot to make the bunk!" cries Sharie, and she climbs back down the companionway.

"Come *on,* honey!" Allen calls down the hatch. "It's two minutes past nine! We're late!"

He turns to the rest of us. "She always keeps me waiting. There are times I'll be in the dory, in the rain, waiting for her, and she's inside fussing about."

"That's how women are," Dag teasingly commiserates. "It's our lot in life to put up with it."

"What's she doing?" cries Allen.

I know what she's doing. She's leaving the bunk the way she likes it to look—the covers smooth, the cushions in place, an inviting, cosy space. It's a ritual, a way of saying goodbye.

Danny starts hoisting the anchor of *Dark Star,* and Gailee sits in the cockpit braiding her long hair, ready for the windy journey. When Sharie appears from the cabin, her eyes are dry and she's smiling. In turn, she and Allen hug me, Dag and Gerry.

"It's your boat now, Gerry," I hear Allen say.

He helps Sharie climb aboard *Dark Star*. She sits next to Gailee in the cockpit, and wraps her red shawl around her. Danny starts the engine, and as *Dark Star* moves away, Sharie blows kisses. Dag, Gerry and I sit on *China Cloud,* watching this departure in tense silence. I've begun to cry; in front of me, I see Gerry wipe his hand across his cheek. Sharie continues to gaze back at her boat, but Allen has already gone below.

"Heading into the future," I murmur to myself. "No lingering over the past."

Then his head pops up from the hatch. "I've left my glasses behind!" he shouts.

Danny motors back while we rush around searching for the spectacles. They're not in the main cabin, and I'm heading into the fore cabin when Danny calls over, "He's found them in his bag!"

Slowly, he steers the boat in a circle around us. This time, Allen stands and looks long and hard at *China Cloud.* His eyes run along the sheer, over the decks, up the masts and the rigging, taking in every detail. Finally he sits down and puts an arm around Sharie. On her face is an expression I saw often during our trip along the coast: an expression that speaks of peace, and fulfilment.

The circle is complete. Allen and Sharie wave one last time at *China Cloud,* then turn to look ahead.

EPILOGUE

■ Early in October 1995 Allen and Sharie flew to Mexico. On arriving in Puerto Vallarta, Allen realized that the country had changed dramatically since they were last there, and that the simple existence he had envisioned was hardly possible anymore. Days later, an earthquake of 7.6 on the Richter scale devastated the area. The village of Melaque, where Allen and Sharie had hoped to spend the winter, was badly damaged. Allen's dream of a new start in Mexico crumbled; barely a week later he and Sharie were back in Canada, living with Allen's sister Kay in West Vancouver.

The following spring, Allen and Sharie returned to Nelson Island, and found a home aboard a small fishing boat in Blind Bay. Sadly, this was to be Sharie's last summer. Her strength ebbed and she grew increasingly frail. In early fall she developed a thrombosis in one leg and was rushed to hospital in Vancouver. She never returned to Blind Bay.

To the end of her life, Sharie remained unfailingly gracious, with a vibrant, enduring spirit. Some weeks before she died, we brought her a copy of the newly published first edition of *Sailing Back in Time*. By then her vision was failing and she could barely recognize the photographs. But she laughed merrily at the stories we read out loud, enjoying the memories of our voyage together. For her the trip had held a special significance, as she knew it was probably the last time she would see many of the places she loved along the coast. Two hours after our final visit with Sharie, on the night of November 29, 1996, she passed away in Allen's arms.

Sharie's death left Allen with a deep, inconsolable loneliness. For a while he stayed with his family, then bought the *Meleet*, a small wooden sailboat, and lived on her in Pender Harbour. But there was only one place where he could begin to find some semblance of peace; aboard *China Cloud*. In the spring of 1998, Gerry Fossum insisted that Allen should move back onto the boat for as long as he wanted. He had worked tirelessly on *China Cloud*, restoring her from stem to stern. He had also installed a head—a flushing toilet—but he knew this was a change that Allen would not view kindly, so he dismantled it and Allen happily went back to using a bucket.

Luna Moth, too, saw some changes. We were often away from home, guiding kayak tours internationally, continuing with our own expeditions and spending long stints in Ireland and England, where Dag worked as a vet. These extended absences meant we were unable to give *Luna Moth* the attention she deserved, so we returned her to Bill Pennell, who owned a half share in her. He removed the troublesome mast and installed an engine; she now lies in Boat Harbour, registered under the name *Egeria Shoals*.

Allen still feels lost without Sharie, but he is more at peace these days, living aboard *China Cloud* in a protected anchorage in False Bay, Lasqueti Island, surrounded by a loving and supportive community. Now almost ninety, he is remarkably fit, maintaining his regime of chin-ups and back exercises, rowing around to visit friends and walking the beaches barefoot, even in the depth of winter. For us, he continues to redefine the meaning of old age.

Maria Coffey and Dag Goering
Protection Island, January 2002

A week before this new edition went to print, Allen Farrell suddenly fell ill with severe pneumonia. He died on the night of March 13, 2002, aged 89. His passing marks the end of an era; without him, this coast will never be the same again. Allen and Sharie touched all who knew them with their compassion and extraordinary generosity. They moved lightly through this world, beacons of harmony and simplicity, and left only beauty in their wake. We miss them greatly, but in our mind's eye we will always see them doing what they loved best: hoisting the sails of *China Cloud* and quietly drifting into the Strait of Georgia—to the waters that sustained them in so many ways during their long, rich lives.

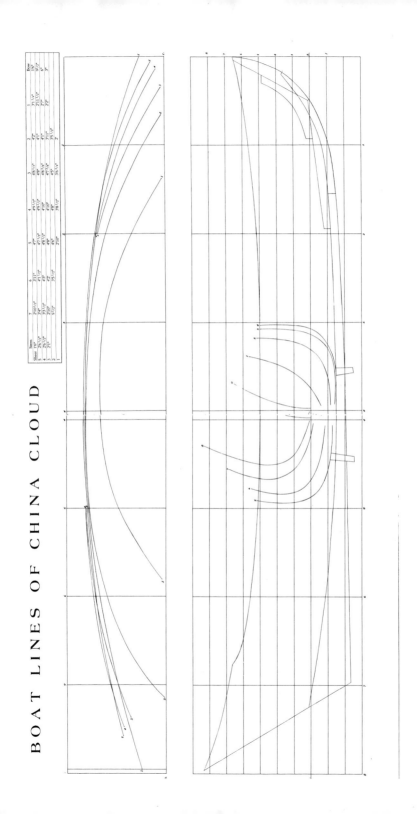

BOAT LINES OF CHINA CLOUD

SAIL PLAN OF CHINA CLOUD

1. bridles
2. parrells
3. hauling parrells–to change the centre of effort of the sail.
4. lazyjacks
5. sail halyard
6. sheets
7. blocks

Length: 42 feet
Beam: 10 feet
Draught: 2 feet 10 inches

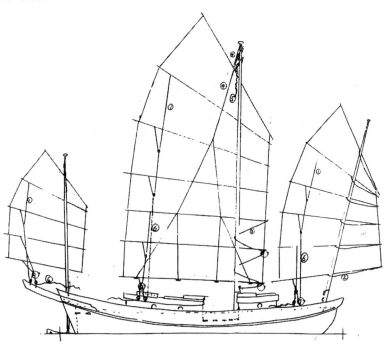

BOAT BUILDING YEARS

Allen Farrell has built over forty boats. Here, in his own words and sketches, are some of them:

Launched 1927, Vancouver
"This was my first boat. I was fourteen years old, and living in West Point Grey, Vancouver. I got an old box and put some sides and the point on it and tarred it up. I didn't get far in it."

Launched 1934, Vancouver
"My first rowboat. I built it on the Burrard Inlet flats for thirteen and a half dollars. I followed some instructions in a magazine, and I copied the lines of a fifteen-foot Norwegian-style boat that I saw on the beach. When I finished the boat Betty and I loaded it with groceries and got a tow up to Smuggler Cove, then over to Lasqueti Island, and fished there all summer."

Launched 1937, Chilliwack
"I had a job in Chilliwack, teaching gymnastics. I thought, it would be so nice to be back on the ocean, so I built a couple of twelve-foot boats. Betty and I had two babies by then.

We put them into apple boxes, took one box each and sailed and rowed the boats down the Fraser River and up to Lasqueti, and fished again."

South Wind

Launched 1938, Vancouver

"She was a thirty-five-foot double-end fish boat, with an old Pontiac engine, and an old water boiler for a gas tank. The gas line kept getting plugged because it was all rusty inside. We got over to Pender Harbour and the engine wouldn't start anymore. I fished out of an eight-foot dinghy for the rest of that year."

Kivi

Launched 1940, Bargain Bay

"She was a twenty-foot cod boat with live wells and an Easthope engine. She had a solid gumwood stem, gumwood cap and gum-wood guard. I kept her pretty nice. That's the boat that Sharie first saw me in. I guess it was *Kivi* that attracted her—all that varnish and white paint."

Wind Song

Launched 1949, Bargain Bay

"She was a thirty-six-foot staysail schooner. We thought she was the best boat we'd ever had, but we're not so sure now, because our ideas on boats have changed. She was a won-derful sea boat. In a following sea, you never had to even touch the tiller, she would just go on her own. In 1951 we went to Hawaii in her, and then Fiji, where we sold her."

Klee Wyck

Launched 1952, Vancouver

"I built her when we came back from Fiji. She was a dainty little boat, five-eighths-inch carvel planked. We went up the coast in her to Nelson Island, and bought ten acres of land on Blind Bay. Later we put a cabin on her, turned her into a cod boat and called her *Grey Gull*."

Ocean Bird

Launched 1958, Blind Bay, Nelson Island

"She was thirty feet long, a gaff cutter. Planked with red cedar on one-inch yellow cedar frames. I built her between making a living and building a house and garden and a breakwater. She took me four years. We sold our place and moved onto her. Then we figured we needed a bigger boat, so we started building *Ocean Girl*."

Ocean Girl

Launched 1960, Oren's Island, Bargain Harbour

"She was a schooner, with squaresails. She was a big heavy boat, forty-five feet long, eleven-eight in the beam and she drew six foot eight. We'd been to England and we'd seen those coasters up in the harbour in Ilfracombe—that's what influenced me. She had big deep bilges and she would heel a bit. We sailed her to Santa Barbara, Acapulco and Hawaii, and around here. Then we decided we needed a smaller boat."

Native Girl

Launched 1965, Green Bay, Nelson Island

"We built *Native Girl* just for the coast, but we did all sorts of voyages in her anyway. She's thirty-nine feet on deck, and started out as a ketch; later I turned her into a schooner. She had red cedar inch-and-a-half planking. Everyone wanted to buy her. When we were in San Diego, there were all these millionaires' boats up on the ways, but everyone came to look at *Native Girl,* not at those big boats."

August Moon

Launched 1973, Lasqueti Island

"She started as a twenty-seven-foot dory, made with half-inch plywood. We rigged her as a lug ketch, with no motor, only oars. We lived on her for a couple of months, and sailed her a little bit, then we bought back *Native Girl* and moved aboard her."

China Cloud

Launched 1982, Scottie Bay, Lasqueti Island

"I thought it would be nice to have a boat to go high and dry in. And junks look so pretty. So I made a model and Sharie saw me and said, 'Oh no, not again!' I made a bottom that wouldn't drag in the water, and I made her light, mainly out of red cedar. The sail area is large compared to her displacement and draught. She's got a nice motion. In a beam sea you can feel her trying to roll and you can feel the bilge keels stopping her. She doesn't heel much because she's got a flat bottom. In a following sea she just skims over the top and there's hardly any roll. She's a different boat, I guess."

ACKNOWLEDGEMENTS

■ To the Farrells' relatives and friends who we met on our voyage, Dag and I extend heartfelt thanks for their warm welcomes, their hospitality, their generous sharing of memories and stories, and for the happy times spent in their company.

Our life aboard *Luna Moth* was made more comfortable by Tom Myers of Cascade Designs, who provided us with mats and sleeping bags and waterproof packs and map cases. Rick Cassels of Mustang Survival provided for our safety and comfort with floater bib-pants and bomber jackets. Our thanks to them, and also to Feathercraft Products Ltd., Soltek Solar Energy Ltd. and Standard Communications for their support.

Help came from many quarters during the process of bringing this book to life. I gratefully acknowledge the Canada Council and the Cultural Services Branch of the Ministry of Small Business, Tourism and Culture for their generous financial assistance. Glenn and Linda Sinclair kindly provided me with a place where I could work without interruption. Dag, as always, was a tremendous support in every sense. Joan Skogan, Carol and Mike Matthews, Margaret Horsfield and Jennifer Nash were great sources of encouragement and inspiration. Jean Blackburn ably helped me with research, and many people, too numerous to list here, patiently answered our queries about coastal history. Dag, Allen and Sharie Farrell and Brian Oltman carefully read and checked the manuscript, and Elaine Jones and Elizabeth McLean gave valuable editorial assistance. To all, very many thanks.

For the use of their photographs we are grateful to Dane Campbell, Collin Hanney, Dale Nordlund and Danny Norrie; we are also grateful to Jimmy Dougan who kindly gave us permission to quote from his song "Southeast" and from *My Daughter's Request,* a book written by his father, the late Charles A. Dougan.

For their encouragement and support at all stages of this project, our thanks to Don Dempster and Judy Batstone.

Above all, Dag and I are indebted to Allen and Sharie Farrell, for their friendship, for the laughter shared and the lessons learned, and for allowing us so intimately into their lives. For all this, and much more, we can never thank them enough.

INDEX

■ Maria Coffey and Dag Goering are an internationally published writer/photographer team and married couple who live on a small island off the west coast of Canada. They have recorded their adventures in four other books: *A Boat in Our Baggage, Three Moons in Vietnam, Jungle Islands* and *Visions of the Wild*. Maria Coffey is also the author of *Fragile Edge, A Lambing Season in Ireland* and three books for children: *A Cat in a Kayak, A Seal in the Family* and *A Cat Adrift*. Their work has appeared in numerous publications including *National Geographic Adventure Magazine, The New York Times, The Globe and Mail, Action Asia, Outdoors Illustrated* and *Sea Kayaker* magazine. Maria and Dag also guide trips world-wide through their adventure travel company, Hidden Places.

For more information on their books and adventures, visit their website, *www.hiddenplaces.net*